The Reference Shelf®

Evolution

Edited by In-Young Chang and Jennifer Curry

Editorial Advisor Lynn M. Messina

The Reference Shelf
Volume 78 • Number 5

The H. W. Wilson Company
2006

The Reference Shelf

The books in this series contain reprints of articles, excerpts from books, addresses on current issues, and studies of social trends in the United States and other countries. There are six separately bound numbers in each volume, all of which are usually published in the same calendar year. Numbers one through five are each devoted to a single subject, providing background information and discussion from various points of view and concluding with a subject index and comprehensive bibliography that lists books, pamphlets, and abstracts of additional articles on the subject. The final number of each volume is a collection of recent speeches, and it contains a cumulative speaker index. Books in the series may be purchased individually or on subscription.

Library of Congress has cataloged this title as follows:

Evolution / [edited by] Jennifer Curry, In-Young Chang.
   p. cm. — (The reference shelf ; 78, no. 5)
     Includes bibliographical references.
   ISBN 0-8242-1063-8 (alk. paper)
   1. Evolution (Biology)   I. Curry, Jennifer, 1977– . II. Chang, In-Young.
   QH366.2.E84595 2006
   576.8—dc22

                               2006024529

Cover: A variety of skulls on display as part of an exhibition on Charles Darwin at the American Museum of Natural History in New York. (DON EMMERT/AFP/Getty Images)

Visit H.W. Wilson's Web site: www.hwwilson.com

Printed in the United States of America

Contents

Preface vii

I. Historical Figures in Evolutionary Biology 1

Editors' Introduction 3
1) The Furtive Evolutionist. Desmond King-Hele. *New Scientist* 5
2) Evolution of a Scientist. Jerry Adler. *Newsweek* 9
3) The Humble Garden Pea Held Secrets of Genetics. Dr. William Reville.
   The Irish Times 16
4) Double-Teaming the Double Helix. Gerald Parshall.
   U.S. News & World Report 19

II. The Political Debate over Evolution 23

Editors' Introduction 25
1) Nearly Two-Thirds of U.S. Adults Believe Human Beings Were
   Created by God: Opinions Are Divided about Evolution Theories.
   The Harris Poll® #52 27
2) Issuing Rebuke, Judge Rejects Teaching of Intelligent Design.
   Laurie Goodstein. *The New York Times*............................. 35
3) Media Coverage of "Intelligent Design." Jason Rosenhouse and
   Glenn Branch. *BioScience*.. 39
4) The Descent of the Straw Man. Denis Boyles. *National Review Online* 51
5) Intelligent Design? Edited by Richard Milner and Vittorio Maestro.
   Natural History 55

III. The Genetic Blueprint 67

Editors' Introduction 69
1) On Darwin's Shoulders. Douglas J. Futuyma. *Natural History*............. 71
2) All in the Family. Thomas Hayden. *U.S. News & World Report* 77
3) Mother Superior. Garry Hamilton. *New Scientist*........................ 81
4) Evo Devo. Gareth Cook. *The Boston Globe*............................. 87
5) Humans, Chimps May Have Bred After Split. Gareth Cook.
   The Boston Globe 91

IV. The Fossil Record 95

Editors' Introduction 97
1) The Fossils Say Yes. Donald R. Prothero. *Natural History* 99

2) Fossil Discovery Fills Gap in Evolutionary Path from Fish to Land Animals.
   Richard Monastersky. *The Chronicle of Higher Education* 105
3) Evolution of Whales. Douglas H. Chadwick. *National Geographic* 107
4) Little Meat-Eater Is No Bird, but Close. William Mullen. *Chicago Tribune*..... 114
5) The Astonishing Micropygmies. Jared Diamond. *Science*................... 117

V. Cognition and Culture.. 121

Editors' Introduction 123
1) Don't Call Me Clever. Simon M. Reader. *New Scientist* 125
2) Who's That Strange Monkey in the Mirror? A Tufted Capuchin Isn't Quite Sure.
   Nicholas Wade. *The New York Times* 131
3) The Morning of the Modern Mind. Kate Wong. *Scientific American* 133
4) Early Chefs Left Indelible Mark on Human Evolution.
   James Randerson. *New Scientist* 143
5) Caveman Crooners May Have Aided Early Human Life. Sharon Begley.
   Associated Press Financial Wire 145

Appendix 149
Was the World Made for Man? Mark Twain............................. 151
Kitzmiller, et al. v. Dover Area School District, et al. 155
Edwards, Governor of Louisiana, et al. v. Aguillard et al. 158

Bibliography 167
Books 169
Web Sites 171
Additional Periodical Articles with Abstracts 173

Index 181

Preface

Few ideas have had as profound an effect on the world as the theory of evolution. In *The Origin of Species*, which Charles Darwin published in 1859, he suggested, contrary to traditional belief, that the Earth's plants and animals were not immutable, or unchanging, and had in fact diverged from other related species, delivering a blow that altered not only humanity's understanding of the natural world but also of our place within it. This explains why a theory that serves as the keystone for modern biology, a theory that is universally accepted within the scientific community, a theory made manifest in this era of genetically modified crops and cattle, continues to raise such controversy with the general public. To acknowledge that humans are subject to the same natural processes as other species suggests the possibility that man is not of divine creation and the world was not, as Mark Twain so succinctly put it, "made for man."[1] The impact of this suggestion on the Victorian mindset must have been akin to the effect that Nicolaus Copernicus's heliocentric model—which placed the sun, not the Earth, at the center of the universe—had on the Church in the 16th century.

A similar breakthrough occurred in 1953, when James Watson and Francis Crick discovered the double helical structure of DNA, illuminating the mechanism by which evolution takes place. Until that point, as Edward J. Larson notes in *Evolution: The Remarkable History of a Scientific Theory*, the gene was a black box and many scientists imagined the gene to be so complex as to require decades to decipher. Watson and Crick determined that the entire genetic code was constructed of four base molecules, which are often represented by the initials: A, T, G, and C. "For those not studying biology at the time in the early 1950s, it is hard to imagine the impact the discovery of DNA had on our understanding of how the world works," the famed zoologist Edward O. Wilson recalled. "If heredity can be reduced to a chain of four molecular letters—granted, billions of such letters to prescribe a whole organism—would it not also be possible to reduce and accelerate the analysis of ecosystems and complex animal behavior?" Indeed, having been provided the means to decipher the "book of life," biologists are rapidly discovering the answers to such age-old questions as what determines an organism's lifespan and whether early humans interbred with Neanderthals.

Given that the process of evolution and our understanding of it are both works in progress, this volume is by no means comprehensive. Rather, it seeks to highlight some of the more important discoveries and debates within the field. The first chapter provides the reader with an overview of evolutionary

---

[1] See Mark Twain's satirical essay on this topic, "Was the World Made for Man?," in the appendix of this book.

theory by presenting biographies of some of the more important figures in its development. For readers interested in the contemporary political debate over teaching evolutionary theory in public schools, the second chapter presents analysis from both sides. The next two sections examine two sources of evidence for various evolutionary theories—the human genome and the fossil record. Finally, the fifth chapter explores the development of higher cognition and culture in human beings and our primate relatives.

In conclusion, we would like to offer our sincere appreciation to the writers and publishers who granted permission to reprint their work. Thanks are also due to the many people who contributed to this book, particularly John Packer, John Farris, David Ramm, Lynn Messina, Paul McCaffrey, Richard Stein, and Albert Rolls.

In-Young Chang and Jennifer Curry
October 2006

I. Historical Figures in Evolutionary Biology

Editors' Introduction

The Scottish historian and social critic Thomas Carlyle, a contemporary of Charles Darwin, once wrote, "The history of the world is but the biography of great men." While the "great man" theory of history has fallen out of favor among academics, it can be useful in tracing the development of the field of evolutionary biology. Though countless scientists have contributed to our understanding of evolution, an examination of the lives of several of its pioneering researchers not only provides an overview of their breakthroughs, but illustrates the resistance they engendered when their findings clashed with cultural assumptions.

Desmond King-Hele's article "The Furtive Evolutionist" illustrates that while Charles Darwin is rightly given credit for having first outlined a theory of evolution, he was not the only naturalist to question the immutability of species. For example, Darwin was quite familiar with the writings of his grandfather, Erasmus Darwin, an early evolutionist whose works are often forgotten. A physician as well as a renowned poet in the deeply religious era of the late 1700s, the elder Darwin relied on his literary credibility to publish *Zoonomia*, a multi-volume medical tome in which he briefly expressed his idea that all life developed over millions of years from microscopic specks, with only the fittest plants and animals surviving. The book was vigorously denounced as blasphemous and subversive, forcing Erasmus Darwin to keep his ideas about evolution private. Nonetheless, he did write a lengthy poem, "The Temple of Nature," which was published posthumously and further elucidated his views on evolutionary theory.

When Charles Darwin began developing his own theory of evolution, he would have known of the censure that his grandfather had received. According to Jerry Adler's biography, "Evolution of a Scientist," Darwin, writing to a friend in 1844, admitted that if he were to publish his ideas—supported by years of careful study and the evidence he had collected while traveling aboard the HMS *Beagle* on a mission to explore the coastal regions of South America and the archipelago of the Galápagos Islands—they would be received as if he were "confessing a murder." In fact, he was induced to publish his seminal work, *On the Origin of Species*, only after he learned that one of his contemporaries, Alfred Russel Wallace, was prepared to put forward a similar theory.

The third biography in this chapter, taken from the *Irish Times*, includes an explanation of the famous study in which the Austrian monk Gregor Mendel quantified the outcome of crossbreeding thousands of carefully selected pea plants. He found that both the dominant and recessive characteristics of parent plants were always present in a resulting hybrid and that the distribution of such characteristics could be predicted through statistics. Although little

3

attention was given to Mendel's findings at the time, his work provided the basis for genetic study in the 20th century and gave further credence to Darwin's theory of evolution.

In "Double-Teaming the Double Helix: J. Watson and F. Crick," Gerald Parshall profiles the work of the scientists James D. Watson and Francis Crick, who delivered "the biggest biological thunderbolt since Darwin," when they discovered the double-helix shape of deoxyribonucleic acid (DNA) molecules in 1953. Their finding led to significant advances in genetics research: once the genetic code was cracked, scientists were able to begin the long and arduous process of deciphering the "book of life."

The Furtive Evolutionist

BY DESMOND KING-HELE
NEW SCIENTIST, APRIL 12, 2003

The year is 1765. The place is Staffordshire, in the heart of England. Horse-drawn wagons trundle along the rutted and pot-holed roads, carrying the pottery and crockery manufactured by Josiah Wedgwood at his factory in Burslem. Breakages are all too frequent. Appalled at these losses, Wedgwood has an ambitious idea. Why not create a smooth liquid road—a canal—to link his manufactory with ports on the coast?

It will require an Act of Parliament, and Wedgwood draws his friends into the campaign. Keenest of them all is Dr Erasmus Darwin, a physician at nearby Lichfield. Darwin writes a pro-canal pamphlet, and also wins over his landowning patients along the route. The canal gets the go-ahead in 1766, and work begins at once, directed by James Brindley. His toughest problem will be the Harecastle tunnel, which will have to be cut through more than 2 kilometres of hard wet rocks. And that's where the picks and shovels of the excavators unearth evolution.

The digging at Harecastle yielded a rich haul of fossils, and in 1767 Josiah Wedgwood sent his friend Erasmus Darwin a big box of bones: after all, doctors knew about bones. But not bones like these. Some of them were huge. Darwin was baffled, and resorted to joking: "The horn is larger than any modern horn I have measured, and must have been that of a Patagonian ox, I believe." It was probably a tusk from an extinct variety of elephant.

After reflecting seriously about the fossils, Darwin soon decided that species must have gradually changed down the ages. He then jumped to what is often called the theory of common descent: that all the life we see today has a common microscopic ancestor—a single "living filament," as Darwin called it. And that filament, he thought, must have originated in the sea.

What an idea. He may have felt like shouting out his evolutionary revelation for all to hear. But he lived only a few steps from Lichfield Cathedral, where a different revelation prevailed: God created species. Anyone who denied that would be shunned by the religious establishment.

So Darwin kept quiet. Then he had another good idea. His family's coat of arms featured three scallop shells. What about adding the motto E conchis omnia, or "everything from shells." He put the motto on his bookplate in 1771. He also had it painted on his carriage, but this was not such a good idea. Canon Seward of Lichfield Cathedral saw the blasphemous words and penned a few satirical lines complaining that Darwin . . .

> ". . . renounces his Creator
> And forms all sense from
>   senseless matter.
> Great wizard he! by magic spells
> Can all things raise from
>   cockle shells."

Darwin was furious. To avoid offending rich patients, however, he had to paint out the motto on his carriage, though he kept the bookplate. He decided to lie low and develop his evolutionary ideas in private.

So all fell quiet in the evolution war. Twenty years later, Darwin, now 60 years old, had been acclaimed as the leading English poet of the day, after the publication of his long poem The Botanic Garden. Even his sharpest critic, Samuel Taylor Coleridge, admitted in 1797 that Darwin was "the first literary character in Europe and the most original-minded Man."

During those 20 years of quiet, Darwin wrote a huge medical tome, which he intended to be published after his death. But his great popularity as a poet emboldened him to publish it while he was still alive. The book was called Zoonomia, and the first volume came out in 1794. Medically, Zoonomia was highly successful, with six American editions and translations into four languages.

But Zoonomia had a wicked sting in the tail. Starting at page 496, Darwin expounded what we now call biological evolution. Species can and do change, he said. Even individual animals changed, "as in the production of the butterfly with painted wings from the crawling caterpillar." Then there were changes produced by "artificial cultivation," as in the various breeds of dogs. Also "monstrosities" (or mutations) were sometimes inherited.

In nature, he said, the changes were driven by "lust, hunger and security." In some species the males had developed weapons such as horns or tusks to combat each other "for the exclusive possession of the females." The outcome of "this contest among the males," Darwin said, was "that the strongest and most active animal should propagate the species, which should thence become improved."

The second urge was hunger, and animals had become adapted to their means of procuring food—parrots "have acquired harder beaks to crack nuts"; others, "as the finches," have beaks for softer seeds. And the need for security had diversified animals' bodies and their colour. He mentioned wings for escape, swiftness of foot, hard shells, camouflage and mimicry.

"Would it be too bold to imagine that all warm-blooded animals have arisen from one living filament?" asked Darwin, "millions of ages" ago. And that the living filament "has been the cause of all organic life?"

By the time Zoonomia came out, Britain was at war with France. The war was going badly in 1797. Britain's navy was beset by mutiny, and the apparently invincible Napoleon had declared his intention to annihilate England. So the government set up a journal to combat subversive ideas, called The Anti-Jacobin, edited by George Canning, a future Prime Minister. Darwin was an obvious target: it was almost treason to suggest that Britons had lower animals, or worse still microscopic specks, as their ancestors. It might even be considered terrorism for this was enough to frighten anyone. In 1798, Canning and two of his cronies wrote a poem called The Loves of the Triangles parodying Darwin's earlier The Loves of the Plants, and added notes rubbishing Darwin's absurd and blasphemous evolutionary ideas.

> *No one spoke up for [Erasmus] Darwin, so he was forced to go underground.*

No one spoke up for Darwin, so he was forced to go underground. And he did so very effectively by dying in 1802, aged 70, leaving another long poem that he called The Origin of Society. His publisher, Joseph Johnson, had been jailed for seditious libel a few years earlier, and prudently changed the title to The Temple of Nature.

This poem and its notes were Darwin's evolutionary testament. He described how life began as microscopic specks in primeval seas and then developed over "millions of ages" (that is, hundreds of millions of years) through fishes, amphibians and eventually land creatures to humankind. He calmly announced all this as if it were a true history, and presented it in vigorous verse thick with facts. Hundreds of lines were devoted to the war in nature, the survival of the fittest among animals and plants, and the non-uniqueness of the human animal:

> "Stoop, selfish Pride! survey thy
>   kindred forms,
> Thy brother-emmets, and thy
>   sister-worms."

The Temple of Nature was a fine achievement. The human genome project, with its percentages for the genes we share with cabbages and worms, shows how right he was—the first person to tell us the truth about where we came from, how we made our way here, and how long it took.

The Temple of Nature was published 200 years ago this month, in April 1803. It deserves a birthday greeting, and much more. Some say it's the most important book on the history of life and society. Others scoff at this, often without having read it. Others still may prefer On the Origin of Species, published 56 years later by Erasmus's grandson Charles. But that is another story.

Evolution of a Scientist

By Jerry Adler
Newsweek, November 28, 2005

On a December night in 1831, HMS Beagle, on a mission to chart the coast of South America, sailed from Plymouth, England, straight into the 21st century. Onboard was a 22-year-old amateur naturalist, Charles Darwin, the son of a prosperous country doctor, who was recruited for the voyage largely to provide company for the Beagle's aloof and moody captain, Robert FitzRoy. For the next five years, the little ship—just 90 feet long and eight yards wide—sailed up and down Argentina, through the treacherous Strait of Magellan and into the Pacific, before returning home by way of Australia and Cape Town. Toward the end of the voyage, the Beagle spent five weeks at the remote archipelago of the Galápagos, home to giant tortoises, black lizards and a notable array of finches. Here Darwin began to formulate some of the ideas about evolution that would appear, a quarter-century later, in "The Origin of Species," which from the day it was written to the present has been among the most influential books ever published. Of the revolutionary thinkers who have done the most to shape the intellectual history of the past century, two—Sigmund Freud and Karl Marx—are in eclipse today, and one—Albert Einstein—has been accepted into the canon of modern thought, even if most people still don't understand what he was thinking. Darwin alone remains unassimilated, provocative, even threatening to some—like Pat Robertson, who recently warned the citizenry of Dover, Pa., that they risked divine wrath for siding with Darwin in a dispute over high-school biology textbooks. Could God still be mad after all this time?

Unintentionally, but inescapably, that is the question raised by a compelling new show that opened Saturday at the American Museum of Natural History in New York. Here are the beetles Darwin collected fanatically, the fossils and ferns he studied obsessively, two live Galápagos tortoises like the ones he famously rode bareback, albeit these were hatched in the Milwaukee County Zoo. And here are the artifacts of his life: his tiny single-shot pistol, his magnifying glass and rock hammer—and the Bible that traveled around the world with him, a reminder that before his voyage he had been studying for the ministry. (Indeed, in a letter to his father, who opposed the trip, he listed all the latter's objections, starting with "disreputable to my character as a clergyman hereafter." Little did he imagine.) The show, which will travel to Boston, Chicago and Toronto before ending its tour in London in Darwin's bicentennial year of 2009, coincides by chance with the publication of two major Darwin anthologies as well as a novel by best-selling author John Darnton, "The Darwin Conspiracy," which playfully inverts history by portraying Darwin as a schemer who dispatched a rival into a volcano and stole the ideas that made him famous. Visitors to Britain will note that Darwin has replaced that other bearded Victorian icon, Charles Dickens, on the British 10-pound note. "Even people who aren't comfortable with Darwin's ideas," says Niles Eldredge, the museum's curator of paleontology, "are fascinated by the man."

In part, the fascination with the man is being driven by his enemies, who say they're fighting "Darwinism," rather than evolution or natural selection. "It's a rhetorical device to make evolution seem like a kind of faith, like 'Maoism'," says Harvard biologist E. O. Wil-

---

"Even people who aren't comfortable with [Charles] Darwin's ideas are fascinated by the man."—Niles Eldredge, curator of paleontology, American Museum of Natural History

---

son, editor of one of the two Darwin anthologies just published. (James D. Watson, codiscoverer of DNA, edited the other, but both include the identical four books.) "Scientists," Wilson adds, "don't call it 'Darwinism'."

But the man is, in fact, fascinating. His own life exemplifies the painful journey from moral certainty to existential doubt that is the defining experience of modernity. He was an exuberant outdoorsman who embarked on one of the greatest adventures in history, but then never again left England. He lived for a few years in London before marrying his first cousin Emma, and moving to a country house where he spent the last 40 years of his life, writing, researching and raising his 10 children, to whom he was extraordinarily devoted. Eldredge demonstrates, in his book accompanying the museum show, "Darwin: Discovering the Tree of Life," how the ideas in "The Origin of Species" took shape in Darwin's notebooks as far back as the 1830s. But he held off publishing until 1859, and then only because he learned that a younger scientist, Alfred Russel Wallace, had come up with a similar theory. Darwin was afflicted throughout his later life by intestinal distress and heart palpitations, which kept him from working for more than a few hours at a time. There are two theories about this mysterious illness: a parasite he picked up in South America, or, as Eldredge believes, anxiety over where his intellectual journey was leading him, and the world.

It appeared to many, including his own wife, that the destination was plainly hell. Emma, who had other plans for herself, was tormented to think they would spend eternity apart.

Darwin knew full well what he was up to; as early as 1844, he famously wrote to a friend that to publish his thoughts on evolution would be akin to "confessing a murder." To a society accustomed to searching for truth in the pages of the Bible, Darwin introduced the notion of evolution: that the lineages of living things change, diverge and go extinct over time, rather than appear suddenly in immutable form, as Genesis would have it. A corollary is that most of the species alive now are descended from one or at most a few original forms (about which he—like biologists even today—has little to say). By itself this was not a wholly radical idea; Darwin's own grandfather, the esteemed polymath Erasmus Darwin, had suggested a variation on that idea decades earlier. But Charles Darwin was the first to muster convincing evidence for it. He had the advantage that by his time geologists had concluded that the Earth was millions of years old (today we know

---

"Man with all his noble qualities . . . still bears in his bodily frame the indelible stamp of his lowly origin."—**Charles Darwin**

---

it's around 4.5 billion); an Earth created on Bishop Ussher's Biblically calculated timetable in 4004 B.C. wouldn't provide the scope necessary to come up with all the kinds of beetles in the world, or even the ones Darwin himself collected. And Darwin had his notebooks and the trunkloads of specimens he had shipped back to England. In Argentina he unearthed the fossil skeleton of a glyptodont, an extinct armored mammal that resembled the common armadillos he enjoyed hunting. The armadillos made, he wrote, "a most excellent dish when roasted in [their] shell," although the portions were small. The glyptodont, by contrast, was close to the size of a hippopotamus. Was it just a coincidence that both species were found in the same place—or could the smaller living animal be descended from the extinct larger one?

But the crucial insights came from the islands of the Galápagos, populated by species that bore obvious similarities to animals found 600 miles away in South America—but differences as well, and smaller differences from one island to another. To Darwin's mind, the obvious explanation was that the islands had been colonized from the mainland by species that then evolved along diverging paths. He learned that it was possible to tell on which island a tortoise was born from its shell. Did God, the supreme intelligence, deign to design distinctive shell patterns for the tortoises of each island?

Darwin's greater, and more radical, achievement was to suggest a plausible mechanism for evolution. To a world taught to see the hand of God in every part of Nature, he suggested a different creative force altogether, an undirected, morally neutral process he called natural selection. Others characterized it as "survival of the fittest," although the phrase has taken on connotations of social and economic competition that Darwin never intended. But he was very much influenced by Thomas Malthus, and his idea that predators, disease and a finite food supply place a limit on populations that would otherwise multiply indefinitely. Animals are in a continuous struggle to survive and reproduce, and it was Darwin's insight that the winners, on average, must have some small advantage over those who fall behind. His crucial insight was that organisms which by chance are better adapted to their environment—a faster wolf, or deer—have a better chance of surviving and passing those characteristics on to the next generation. (In modern terms, we would say pass on their *genes*, but Darwin wrote long before the mechanisms of heredity were understood.) Of course, it's not as simple as a one-dimensional contest to outrun the competition. If the climate changes, a heavier coat might represent the winning edge. For a certain species, intelligence has been a useful trait. Evolution is driven by the accumulation of many such small changes, culminating in the emergence of an entirely new species. "[F]rom the war of nature, from famine and death, the most exalted object which we are capable of conceiving, namely, the production of the higher animals, directly follows," Darwin wrote.

And there was an even more troubling implication to his theory. To a species that believed it was made in the image of God, Darwin's great book addressed only this one cryptic sentence: "Much light will be thrown on the origin of man and his history." That would come 12 years later, in "The Descent of Man," which explicitly linked human beings to the rest of the animal kingdom by way of the apes. "Man may be excused for feeling some pride at having risen, though not through his own exertions, to the very summit of the organic scale," Darwin wrote, offering a small sop to human vanity before his devastating conclusion: "that man with all his noble qualities . . . still bears in his bodily frame the indelible stamp of his lowly origin."

So it was apparent to many even in 1860—when the Anglican Bishop Samuel Wilberforce debated Darwin's defender Thomas Huxley at Oxford—that Darwin wasn't merely contradicting the literal Biblical account of a six-day creation, which many educated Englishmen of his time were willing to treat as allegory. His ideas, carried to their logical conclusion, appeared to undercut the very basis of Christianity, if not indeed all theistic religion. Was the entire panoply of life stretching back millions of years to its single-celled origins, with its innumerable extinctions and branchings, really just a prelude and backdrop to the events of the Bible? When did *Homo sapiens*, descended by a series of tiny changes in an unbroken line from earlier species of apes, develop a soul? The British biologist Richard Dawkins, an outspoken defender of Darwin and a nonbeliever, famously wrote that evolution "made it possible to be an intellectually fulfilled atheist." Although Darwin struggled with questions of faith his whole life, he ultimately described himself as an "Agnostic." But he reached that conclusion through a different, although well-traveled, route. William Howarth, an environmental historian who teaches a course at Princeton called "Darwin in Our Time," dates Darwin's doubts about Christianity to his encounters with slave-owning Christians—some of them no doubt citing Scripture as justification—which deeply offended Darwin, an ardent abolitionist. More generally, Darwin was troubled by theodicy, the problem of evil: how could a benevolent and omnipotent God permit so much suffering in the world he created? Believers argue that human suffering is ennobling, an agent of "moral improvement," Darwin acknowledged. But with his intimate knowledge of beetles, frogs, snakes and the rest of an omnivorous, amoral creation, Darwin wasn't buying it. Was God indifferent to "the suffering of millions of the lower animals throughout almost endless time"? In any case, it all changed for him after 1851. In that year Darwin's beloved eldest daughter, Annie, died at the age of 10—probably from tuberculosis—an instance of suffering that only led him down darker paths of despair.

A legend has grown up that Darwin experienced a deathbed conversion and repentance for his life's work, but his family has always denied it. He did, however, manage to pass through the needle's eye of Westminster Abbey, where he was entombed with honor in 1882.

So it's not surprising that, down to the present day, fundamentalist Christians have been suspicious of Darwin and his works—or that in the United States, where 80 percent of the population believe God created the universe, less than half believe in evolution. Some believers have managed to square the circle by mapping out separate realms for science and religion. "Science's proper role is to explore natural explanations for the material world," says the biologist Francis Collins, director of the Human Genome Project and an evangelical Christian. "Science provides no answers to the question 'Why are we here, anyway?' That is the role of philosophy and theology." The late Stephen Jay Gould, a prolific writer on evolution and a religious agnostic, took the same approach. But, as Dawkins tirelessly observes, religion makes specific metaphysical claims that appear to conflict with those of evolution. Dealing with those requires some skill in Biblical interpretation. In mainstream Christian seminaries the dominant view, according to Holmes Rolston III, a philosopher at Colorado State University and author of "Genes, Genesis and God," is that the Biblical creation story is a poetic version of the scientific account, with vegetation and creatures of the sea and land emerging in the same basic order. In this interpretation, God gives his creation a degree of autonomy to develop on its own. Rolston points to Genesis 1:11, where God, after creating the heavens and the Earth, says, "Let the Earth put forth vegetation . . ." "You needed a good architect at the big bang to get the universe set up right," he says. "But the account describes a God who opens up possibilities in which creatures are generated in an Earth that has these rich capacities."

Collins identifies the soul with the moral law, the uniquely human sense of right and wrong. "The story of Adam and Eve can thus be interpreted as the description of the moment at which this moral law entered the human species," he says. "Perhaps a certain threshold of brain development had to be reached before this became possible—but in my view the moral law itself defies a purely biological explanation."

The Darwin exhibit was conceived in 2002, when the current round of Darwin-bashing was still over the horizon, but just in those three years' time museum officials found they had to greatly expand their treatment of the controversy—in particular, the rise of "intelligent design" as an alternative to natural selection. ID posits a supernatural force behind the emergence of complex biological systems—such as the eye—composed of many interdependent parts. Although ID advocates have struggled to achieve scientific respectability, biologists overwhelmingly dismiss it as nonsense. Collins comments, in a video that is part of the museum show: "[ID] says, if there's some part of science that you can't understand, that must be where God is. Historically, that hasn't gone well. And if science does figure out [how the eye evolved]—and I believe it's very likely that science will . . . then where is God?"

Where is God? It is the mournful chorus that has accompanied every new scientific paradigm over the last 500 years, ever since Copernicus declared him unnecessary to the task of getting the sun up into the sky each day. The church eventually reconciled itself to the reality of the solar system, which Darwin, perhaps intentionally, invoked in the stirring conclusion to the "Origin": "There is grandeur in this view of life . . . that whilst this planet has gone cycling on according to the fixed law of gravity, from so simple a beginning endless forms most beautiful and most wonderful have been, and are being, evolved." For all his nets and guns and glasses, Darwin never found God; by the same token, the Bible has nothing to impart about the genetic relationships among the finches he did find. But it is human nature to seek both kinds of knowledge. Perhaps after a few more cycles of the planet, we will find a way to pursue them both in peace.

Never a Dull Moment

From the start, the theory of evolution has provoked challenges rooted in religion.

1860

The "Great Debate"
Bishop Samuel Wilberforce leads an attack on Darwin. Two of England's leading scientists, Thomas Huxley and Joseph Hooker, fiercely support Darwin's work.

1882

Darwin Dies
The scientist is buried with honor in Westminster Abbey, a few feet from Sir Isaac Newton. England's leading scientists, clergy and politicians attend the funeral.

1925

The "Monkey Trial"
Tennessee teacher John Scopes is convicted of violating a state law prohibiting the instruction of evolution. The result galvanizes evolution proponents.

1948

Public-School Shift
The Supreme Court bans religious instruction in public schools, noting that the First Amendment requires the separation of church and state.

1960s

Teaching Reaffirmed
The Supreme Court, headed by Chief Justice Earl Warren, rules that an Arkansas law prohibiting the teaching of evolution violates the First Amendment.

1981–1982

Creationism Returns
Arkansas passes the Balanced Treatment for Creation-Science and Evolution-Science Act. The act is declared unconstitutional the following year.

1980s

Intelligent Design
Some U.S. proponents of creationism begin to promote the idea that the complexity of living organisms shows life was created by an "intelligent designer."

1996

A Pope Speaks
Stating that evolution is "more than a hypothesis," John Paul II proclaims there is no essential conflict between Darwin's theory and Catholicism.

2000 to Now

Current Opinion
Less than half of all Americans believe in evolution. Meanwhile, in England, Darwin is honored with a portrait on the 10-pound note.

The Humble Garden Pea Held
Secrets of Genetics

By Dr. William Reville
The Irish Times, September 22, 1997

This year marks the 175th anniversary of the birth of the great Austrian scientist monk Gregor Mendel, who is venerated as the father of modern genetics.

Mendel was born in 1822 of peasant parents in Moravia (now part of Czechoslovakia). He studied for a short period at the Institute of Olmutz, but had to leave for financial reasons, and became an Augustinian monk at the monastery at Brno.

He studied mathematics and natural history in Vienna to become a high school science teacher in Brno. In his spare time he studied the results of making crosses between different varieties of garden peas.

Mendel's interest had been sparked by observations of the results of the hybridisation of ornamental plants to produce new varieties. He noted the regularity of the results and he wondered what would happen if the hybrids were crossed.

Garden peas were available in pure-breeding varieties. They reproduce sexually and the reproductive organs are enclosed within the petals so that self-pollination (fertilisation) normally takes place. However, the plants can easily be cross-pollinated artificially.

Mendel studied 22 varieties in experiments extending over eight years. To illustrate some of the results he achieved let us consider his studies concerning the position of the pea-flowers on the stem.

Mendel used two varieties of pure-breeding plants. In one variety the flowers always had an axial distribution, i.e., along the main stem. In the other variety the flowers always had a terminal distribution, i.e., bunched at the top of the stem.

Mendel cross-pollinated the two varieties and examined the progeny—called the F1 generation. The parent plants are called the P1 generation.

The cross-pollination was carried out as follows. The male and female sex organs of the plant are enclosed within the flower. The tip of the male organ is called the anther, which produces the male sex cell—the pollen. The pistil produces the egg cell.

Mendel removed the anthers of an immature flower of one variety and covered the flower with a small bag to prevent stray pollen from landing. When the female portion was mature, Mendel transferred pollen from the alternative variety and again covered it.

He found that all the plants in the F1 generation were of the axial flower variety.

To find what had happened to the hereditary factor for terminal flowers, Mendel allowed self-pollination of the F1 plants to produce second-generation (F2) plants. In this generation he found that some of the plants were of the terminal flower variety. The ratio of plants with axial flowers to plants with terminal flowers was 3 to 1 (actually 3.14 to 1).

Mendel reasoned that there are two factors in each plant for flower position, but only one of the two factors is carried by a pollen grain or an egg. When pollination occurs, the number of factors is restored to two.

The pure-breeding P1 plants with axial flowers contained two factors for the axial position. The pure-breeding P1 plants with terminal flowers contained two factors for the terminal position.

The plants in the F1 generation contained both factors, but all of these plants had axial flowers. Therefore, the factor for axial position must be dominant over the factor for terminal position, which Mendel termed a recessive factor. When F1 generation pollen grains and eggs are formed, some carry the factor for axial flower position and some the factor for terminal position. If these plants are allowed to self-fertilise, it will produce a random mixture of the two factors.

Some seeds get two factors for axial position, some get a factor of each kind, and some get two factors for terminal flowers. Mendel calculated by mathematical probability that one quarter of F2 plants would be of the first kind, one half of the second kind, and one quarter of the third kind.

The factor for axial flowers is dominant. Therefore the first two groups have axial flowers and only the third group has terminal flowers, i.e., three fourths of the plants should have axial flowers and one fourth should have terminal flowers. Mendel got an experimental ratio of 3.14 to 1, very close to the mathematical expectations.

Apart from flower position, Mendel used six other pairs of alternative traits in his experiments (e.g., round and wrinkled seeds, long and short stems etc), and found that all behaved in the same manner, i.e., gave a three to one ratio of dominant to recessive traits in the F2 generation. Each of the ratios differed slightly from three to one, but not enough to raise any serious doubts.

Mendel used large numbers of F2 plants, which was very important. Had he used smaller numbers the results might have deviated more from the mathematical expectation. Such results would be difficult to analyse.

In his experiments, across all seven pairs of traits, Mendel made 14,889 observations of dominant traits and 5,010 observations of recessive traits in the F2 generation—a ratio of 2.98 to 1, which is as close to a three to one ratio as you could hope to achieve under experimental conditions where chance assortment is involved.

The modern word for Mendel's factors is *genes*. Mendel's interpretation for what happens in such a cross is today accepted as the correct analysis not only for plants but also for animals.

Mendel's system was to represent dominant genetic factors using a capital letter for the dominant gene and the same letter in the lower case for the recessive alternative. The letter is the first letter in the trait which is less common.

For flower position, T means axial and t means terminal. That nomenclature is still in use today, e.g., h for the haemophilia gene (bleeder's disease) and H for the alternative dominant gene that is associated with normal blood-clotting.

> *Until Mendel's brilliant work nobody understood the mechanism of inheritance.*

Of course, it has been known from time immemorial that characteristics are inherited from generation to generation, but until Mendel's brilliant work nobody understood the mechanism of inheritance. Mendel's identification of the fundamental factors that determine an organism's characteristics and how these factors (genes) can independently sort and segregate from generation to generation was a revolutionary breakthrough.

Mendel reported his results at a meeting of the Association for Natural Research in Brno in 1865 and published the work that same year in a book under the title *Treatises on Plant Hybrids*. The work was ahead of its time and was not appreciated by the wider scientific community (nor indeed was it widely read).

In 1900 there was a famous rediscovery and appreciation of Mendel's work by Carl Correns in Germany, Hugo de Vries in Holland and Erich von Tschermak-Seysenegg in Austria.

Mendel's work laid the firm foundation for the modern science of genetics. The rise of molecular biology in this century identified the chemical nature of the gene as DNA and demonstrated how the gene determines characteristics—by controlling and specifying what proteins are synthesised. We are now in the middle of a spectacular explosion of genetic-based developments.

Mendel's experiments stand up. He achieved almost perfect results because he was simply that good. Pure genius.

Mendel was disheartened by the lack of response to his published work. He was elected as abbot of the monastery in 1868. The heavy workload of running the monastery took him away from his beloved experiments.

Shortly before his death in 1883 he said: "My scientific studies have afforded me great gratification, and I am convinced it will not be long before the whole world acknowledges the results of my work." Seventeen years later his prediction came true.

Double-Teaming the Double Helix

By Gerald Parshall
U.S. News & World Report, August 17–24, 1998

"We wish to suggest a structure for the salt of deoxyribose nucleic acid (DNA)," the article in the April 25, 1953, issue of Nature began. "This structure has novel features which are of considerable biological interest." In the sedate tone required for a professional journal, two decidedly unsedate scientists were delivering the biggest biological thunderbolt since Darwin. James Watson, an American only 23 years old, and Francis Crick, a Brit still shy of a Ph.D., had penetrated the secret of life, discovering the structure of the molecule that carries inherited traits. The legend of their Nobel Prize–winning triumph, achieved in a very short time in a fit of inspiration, would grow for years before gathering a bit of tarnish. "Honest Jim" Watson (as some colleagues dubbed him unkindly) and Crick had gotten a crucial assist from another scientist, whose work was shown to them without her permission. Her name was Rosalind Franklin, and she went to her grave never learning what had happened.

Watson and Crick's breakthrough rested on a brilliant interpretation of other people's research, published and unpublished. Watson was a child prodigy from Chicago, a former Quiz Kid on the radio who had earned his Ph.D. in genetics from Indiana University at age 22. Crick, trained as a physicist and 12 years older than Watson, was seeking his Ph.D. in the X-ray studies of protein. They met in the fall of 1951 when Watson arrived at Cavendish Laboratory at Cambridge on a fellowship, eager to pursue girls, the nature of DNA, and fame. Crick, who had lately remarried, was equally committed at least to the second of these interests, and he was not averse to pursuit of the third. The wisecracking, bumptious Watson bonded instantly with the ever exuberant Crick, whose booming laugh warned of his approach like a foghorn. The two were put into an office together well away from others so that their boisterous communion would cause no general disturbance.

Although most biologists thought genes were made up of proteins, Watson and Crick were among those who believed DNA held the key. They were determined to build a model of a DNA molecule. Never mind that both were supposed to be working on other projects. An even bigger obstacle loomed—they were barred from doing original research. The DNA molecule was too small to be viewed by microscope; it could be "seen" only by X-raying it in crystallized form, which yielded shadowy pictures. British science had assigned such studies exclusively to King's College in London. Earlier, Watson had hoped (as he would write years later) that a job offer from King's might grow out of the apparent attraction of a King's scientist, Maurice Wilkins, to Watson's comely sister. But romance did not blossom.

Photo Reconnaissance.

Before Watson and Crick could have a go at building a DNA model, they needed to know what the King's College X-rays were revealing. In a seeming stroke of luck, Franklin, the best of the crystallographers, lectured on her findings in November 1951. Her tentative conclusion: The DNA molecule was a "big helix" with a sugar-phosphate backbone on the outside. Watson attended the talk but took no notes and disastrously misremembered important parts of what Franklin said. Watson and Crick spent 24 hours building a three-chain DNA model with the backbone on the inside. The next day they showed it to Franklin and to Wilkins with an air of proud expectancy. Franklin quickly deflated them; to begin with, their model provided only a tiny fraction of the necessary water content. When word of the fiasco reached Sir Lawrence Bragg, the head of Cavendish Laboratory, he ordered Watson and Crick to leave DNA to the King's researchers.

Before Watson and Crick could have a go at building a DNA model, they needed to know what the King's College X-rays were revealing.

For the next year, they did. Crick worked mostly on his doctorate, Watson devoted himself mostly to "sex" (as he liked to say). He was studying the mating of bacteria. In January 1953, one of the world's most gifted chemists, Linus Pauling, who had discovered the structure of the protein molecule, published a paper proposing a structure for DNA. Watson and Crick felt sure their avenue to fame was about to close. But it turned out that Pauling's model was shot through with errors; Watson and Crick toasted his failure at a pub and immediately began worrying that his mortification would make him hellbent to return to the problem and get it right. Unless they did so first.

Doing that would require at least a peek at the King's College X-ray pictures. Unlike the Watson-Crick team, the Franklin-Wilkins team at King's was no "team" at all. Although King's had hired Franklin as an independent researcher, Wilkins treated her like an assistant. Franklin rebelled (she was incensed by the college's discrimination against female scientists; they could not, for example, have lunch with male colleagues in the main dining room). She refused to share data with Wilkins unless he accepted her as an equal. Watson had cultivated Wilkins for months, sympathizing with his complaints of Franklin's stubbornness. When Watson came calling in January 1953, Wilkins revealed he had been quietly copying Franklin's data. He showed Watson one of her X-ray photos. It made his mouth fall open and his pulse race. While on the train back to Cambridge, Watson sketched the image in the margin of a newspaper. It confirmed that the molecule was a helix. Watson concluded it was likely made up of two chains of DNA.

Watson and Crick went into a frenzy of model building. The object was to order the atoms within the molecule in a way that provided for replication while remaining consistent with the known rules of chemistry. After their first model with the sugar-phosphate backbone on the inside failed, they put the backbone on the outside (as per Franklin's 1951 lecture). Trial and error ultimately produced a sequence that worked—a complementary pairing of the four nitrogen bases in each DNA strand. Watson and Crick stood at last before a model of the mechanism by which genes copy themselves. It was March 7, 1953. Later at lunch at the Eagle pub, Crick announced to all that he and his confrere had found "the secret of life." The other patrons, many nursing glasses of dark beer, had heard that claim before.

Postscript

Watson and Crick achieved fame and went on to distinguished careers. Watson taught at Harvard University for 21 years, became director of the Cold Spring Harbor Laboratory of Quantitative Biology on Long Island, and headed the National Institutes of Health's Human Genome project—mapping human genes—between 1988 and 1992. Crick taught at Cambridge University for two decades and then settled in at the Salk Institute for Biological Studies in La Jolla, Calif. Rosalind Franklin died of cancer in 1958 at age 37. Had she lived, she might have shared the Nobel Prize with Watson and Crick in 1962. The Nobel Prize, however, is not given to the dead. Or to the unlucky. As it happened, Maurice Wilkins was the third honoree. The Nobel committee credited him with Franklin's stellar DNA work as well as his own.

Milestones

By Ellen F. Licking

1966

The genetic code is cracked. Scientists can now begin to read the blue-prints of all organisms.

1972–73

Scientists begin splicing pieces of DNA together, forming genes called recombinant molecules and launching the biotechnology revolution. Human genes can now be spliced into bacteria, which churn out human proteins.

1977

Frederick Sanger reveals for the first time the complete genetic information of a micro-organism, paving the way for the human genome project, expected to map all human genes by 2003.

1981

Researchers create the first transgenic animal, inserting a viral gene into the DNA of a mouse. Such creatures, carrying human genes, serve as models for studying human diseases.

1984

Biologist and surfer Kary Mullis invents the polymerase chain reaction, PCR, a new method of sequencing DNA. It speeds along all genetic research, including the identification of criminals from samples of DNA.

1997

The lamb Dolly, first mammal cloned from an adult cell, is born in Scotland. Forecasts of human clones stir intense ethical debate.

II. The Political Debate over Evolution

Editors' Introduction

"**P**eople of goodwill wish to see science and religion at peace, working together to enrich our practical and ethical lives," the influential evolutionary biologist Stephen Jay Gould wrote in *Rocks of Ages: Science and Religion in the Fullness of Life.* The key to avoiding the sort of rancorous public debate that has beleaguered evolutionary biology, he argued, is to resign each institution to separate and nonoverlapping magisterium (or fields of study), with science serving its purpose to document and explain the "factual character of the natural world" and religion operating in the "equally important, but utterly different realm of human purposes, meanings, and values." According to Gould, "If religion can no longer dictate the nature of factual conclusions residing properly with the magisterium of science, then scientists cannot claim higher insight into moral truth from any superior knowledge of the world's empirical constitution. This mutual humility leads to important practical consequences in a world of such diverse passions. We would do well to embrace the principle and enjoy the consequences."

Conflict arises, however, when people blur the lines of this division—as in the case of creationism, which Gould described as a "distinctively American violation" of his idea of nonoverlapping magisterium. This doctrine holds to the biblical description of creation, which runs counter to the central tenants of the scientific method, requiring that all claims about the physical world be supported by empirical evidence and be verifiable through experimentation. Nonetheless, conservative partisans have tried for decades to impose creationism on the science curriculum in public schools. While most Americans are familiar with the Scopes trial (made famous by the play and film *Inherit the Wind*), the debate over creationism—or, at least, its role in public education—was settled in 1987 by the Supreme Court case *Edwards v. Aguillard.*[1] The Court found that a Louisiana law requiring "creation science" to be taught alongside evolutionary theory was unconstitutional because it was intended to advance a particular religious belief. In recent years opponents of evolutionary theory have adopted a new strategy, insisting that classroom time be allocated for the theory of "intelligent design" (ID), which asserts that species do evolve slightly over time but that the complexity of natural phenomena cannot be explained by evolution alone, thereby proving the existence of a higher being or designer. The intelligent design movement was recently dealt a blow, however, in the U.S. District Court ruling of *Kitzmiller v. Dover Area School*

---

[1] An excerpt from the ruling in *Edwards v. Aguillard* is included in the appendix of this book.

District (2005); the presiding judge, John E. Jones, found that intelligent design did not qualify as science, and "moreover that ID cannot uncouple itself from its creationist, and thus religious, antecedents."[2]

The debate over evolution, though not unique to the United States, has held more sway here than in European nations, where the theory is largely accepted as a fact. The 2005 Harris Interactive poll titled "Nearly Two-thirds of U.S. Adults Believe Human Beings Were Created by God," the first entry in this chapter, reveals that the theory of evolution is losing ground with the American public. In 1994, 44 percent of those polled agreed that "human beings developed from earlier species." As of June 2005, only 38 percent of respondents agreed with that statement.

While most respondents to the Harris Poll—55 percent—felt that creationism and intelligent design should be taught alongside evolution in public schools, the courts have repeatedly affirmed that teaching creationism violates the separation of church and state. In the second article in this chapter, "Issuing Rebuke, Judge Rejects Teaching of Intelligent Design," from the *New York Times*, Laurie Goodstein reports on Judge John E. Jones's historic decision, in which he ruled that intelligent design, like creationism, advances "a particular version of Christianity," thereby also violating the separation of church and state.

In "Media Coverage of 'Intelligent Design,'" Jason Rosenhouse and Glenn Branch examine the accuracy of the media's reporting on the evolution–versus–intelligent design debate. They note that reporters with little or no scientific training often report on evolution-creationism controversies, leading to misrepresentations of the arguments that color the wider public debate. Shortcomings are found in deeply partisan cable news programs, as well as media outlets concerned with providing equal time to biologists and creationists. The authors maintain that news outlets that offer equal coverage to both sides of this divisive issue can give viewers the false sense that both are equally respected in the scientific community. They conclude with suggestions on how scientists might work more constructively with the media in the heated evolution debate.

Writing for *National Review Online*, Denis Boyles argues in "The Descent of the Straw Man" that—dating back to the Scopes trial—liberals have used the controversy surrounding evolution to depict "conservatives as zealots and simpletons." He argues that the debate has also revealed the anti-religious bigotry of some secularists: as an example, he relates the story of a religious studies professor at the University of Kansas who stirred up a controversy after posting derogatory remarks about fundamentalist Christians on the Web site for an organization of atheist and agnostic students.

The final selection in this chapter, "Intelligent Design?" provides statements from three leading proponents of intelligent design along with three responses from supporters of Darwinian evolution. The article also includes an overview of the debate.

---

[2] An excerpt from the ruling in *Kitzmiller v. Dover Area School District* is included in the appendix of this book.

Nearly Two-Thirds of U.S. Adults Believe Human Beings Were Created by God

Opinions Are Divided about Evolution Theories

THE HARRIS POLL® #52, JULY 6, 2005

Earlier this year, the State Board of Education in Kansas reignited an old debate—whether or not creationism should be taught in public schools—and shone the spotlight on a new theory, intelligent design. While many in the scientific community may question why this issue has been raised again, a new national survey shows that almost two-thirds of U.S. adults (64%) agree with the basic tenet of creationism, that "human beings were created directly by God."

At the same time, approximately one-fifth (22%) of adults believe "human beings evolved from earlier species" (evolution) and 10 percent subscribe to the theory that "human beings are so complex that they required a powerful force or intelligent being to help create them" (intelligent design). Moreover, a majority (55%) believe that all three of these theories should be taught in public schools, while 23 percent support teaching creationism only, 12 percent evolution only, and four percent intelligent design only.

These are some of the results of a nationwide Harris Poll of 1,000 U.S. adults surveyed by telephone by Harris Interactive® between June 17 and 21, 2005.

Other key findings include:

- A majority of U.S. adults (54%) *do not* think human beings developed from earlier species, up from 46 percent in 1994.

- Forty-nine percent of adults believe plants and animals have evolved from some other species while 45 percent do not believe that.

- Adults are evenly divided about whether or not apes and man have a common ancestry (46 percent believe we do and 47 percent believe we do not).

- Again divided, 46 percent of adults agree that "Darwin's theory of evolution is proven by fossil discoveries," while 48 percent disagree.

Factors such as age, education, political outlook, and region appear to guide views on this debate.

- In general, older adults (those 55 years of age and older), adults without a college degree, Republicans, conservatives, and Southerners are more likely to embrace the creationism positions in the questions asked.

- Those with a college education, Democrats, independents, liberals, adults aged 18 to 54 and those from the Northeast and West support the belief in evolution in larger numbers. However, among these groups, majorities believe in creationism.

- Despite the significant numbers who believe in creationism, pluralities among the demographic subgroups examined still believe all three concepts (evolution, creationism, and intelligent design) should be taught in public schools

Methodology

The Harris Poll® was conducted by telephone within the United States between June 17 and 21, 2005 among a nationwide cross section of 1,000 adults (aged 18 and over). Figures for sex, race, education, and region were weighted where necessary to align them with their actual proportions in the population.

In theory, with a probability sample of this size, one can say with 95 percent certainty that the overall results have a sampling error of plus or minus 3 percentage points of what they would be if the entire U.S. adult population had been polled with complete accuracy. Sampling error for the sub-sample results (as shown in the tables above) is higher and varies. Unfortunately, there are several other possible sources of error in all polls or surveys that are probably more serious than theoretical calculations of sampling error. They include refusals to be interviewed (nonresponse), question wording and question order, interviewer bias, weighting by demographic control data and screening (e.g., for likely voters). It is impossible to quantify the errors that may result from these factors.

These statements conform to the principles of disclosure of the National Council on Public Polls.

Table 1

Did Humans Develop from Earlier Species?

"Do you think human beings developed from earlier species?"

Base: All Adults

	March 1994	June 2005
	%	%
Yes, I think human beings developed from earlier species.	44	38
No, I do not think human beings developed from earlier species.	46	54
Not sure/Decline to answer	11	8

Note: Percentages may not add up exactly to 100 due to rounding

Table 2

Plant and Animal Development from Other Species

"Do you believe all plants and animals have evolved from other species or not?"

Base: All Adults

	June 2005
	%
Yes, I believe plants and animals have evolved from some other species.	49
No, I do not believe plants and animals have evolved from some other species.	45
Not sure/Decline to answer	7

Note: Percentages may not add up exactly to 100 due to rounding

Table 3

Do Man and Apes Have Common Ancestry?

"Do you believe apes and man have a common ancestry or not?"

Base: All Adults

	July 1996	June 2005
	%	%
Yes, apes and man do have a common ancestry.	51	46
No, apes and man do not have a common ancestry.	43	47
Not sure/Decline to answer	5	7

Note: Percentages may not add up exactly to 100 due to rounding

Table 4

Darwin's Theory of Evolution Proven by Fossil Discoveries?

"Please tell me whether you agree or disagree witht he following statement: Darwin's theory of evolution is proven by fossil discoveries."

Base: All Adults

	January 2004	June 2005
	%	%
Agree (NET)	43	46
Strongly agree	19	15
Somewhat agree	24	30
Disagree (NET)	51	48
Somewhat disagree	16	19
Strongly disagree	35	29
Not Sure/Decline to answer	6	6

Table 5

Where Humans Come From

"Which of the following do you believe about how human beings came to be?"

Base: All Adults

	June 2005
	%
Human beings evolved from earlier species.	22
Human beings were created directly by God.	64
Human beings are so complex that they required a powerful force or intelligent being to help create them.	10
Not sure/Decline to answer	4

Table 6

Evolution in the Classroom

"Regardless of what you may personally believe should be taught in public schools?"

Base: All Adults

	June 2005
	%
Evolution only: "Evolution says that human beings evolved from earlier stages of animals."	12
Creationism only: "Creationism says that human beings were created directly by God."	23
Intelligent design only: "Intelligent design says that human beings are so complex that they required a powerful force or intelligent being to help create them."	4
All three	55
Neither	3
Not sure/Decline to answer	3

Table 7

Summary of Key Questions about Human Evolution—By Education

Base: All Adults

	All Adults (n=1,000)	Education			
		H.S. or Less (n=407)	Some College (n=339)	College Grad (n=157)	Post Grad (n=75)
	%	%	%	%	%
Human Development from Earlier Species					
Yes	38	32	35	46	60
No	54	59	56	46	33
PLANT AND ANIMAL DEVELOPMENT					
Yes	49	44	48	55	65
No	45	48	45	39	32
MAN AND APES HAVE COMMON ANCESTRY					
Yes	46	46	41	53	57
No	47	47	50	39	40
DARWIN'S THEORY OF EVOLUTION PROVEN BY FOSSIL EVIDENCE					
Yes	46	40	44	55	64
No	48	51	51	39	34
HUMAN EVOLUTION					
Belief in evolution	22	17	21	31	35
Belief in creationism	64	73	66	48	42
Belief in intelligent design	10	6	10	15	17

Table 8

Summary of Key Questions about Human Evolution—By Party and Political Philosophy

Base: All Adults

	All Adults (n=1,000)	Part; ID			Political Philosophy		
		Republican (n=351)	Democrat (n=439)	Independent (n=170)	Conservative (n=533)	Moderate (n=103)	Liberal (n=359)
	%	%	%	%	%	%	%
HUMAN DEVELOPMENT FROM EARLIER SPECIES							
Yes	38	27	48	36	25	40	56
No	54	65	44	53	65	52	37
PLANT AND ANIMAL DEVELOPMENT							
Yes	49	37	61	47	38	50	65
No	45	58	33	42	53	46	31
MAN AND APES HAVE COMMON ANCESTRY							
Yes	46	30	61	44	37	36	63
No	47	62	32	47	56	52	31
DARWIN'S THEORY OF EVOLUTION PROVEN BY FOSSIL EVIDENCE							
Yes	46	37	55	43	36	40	62
No	48	58	40	45	58	43	35
HUMAN EVOLUTION							
Belief in evolution	22	16	27	25	16	22	32
Belief in creationism	64	73	58	57	75	63	48
Belief in intelligent design	10	9	11	7	7	4	

Table 9

Summary of Key Questions about Human Evolution—By Age and Region

Base: All Adults

	All Adults (n=1,000)	Age			Region			
		18-34 (n=258)	35-54 (n=374)	55+ (n=340)	Northeast (n=213)	Midwest (n=220)	South (n=349)	West (n=218)
	%	%	%	%	%	%	%	%
HUMAN DEVELOPMENT FROM EARLIER SPECIES								
Yes	38	46	38	29	52	37	28	41
No	54	46	53	61	38	57	64	50
PLANT AND ANIMAL DEVELOPMENT								
Yes	49	51	50	46	63	47	41	51
No	45	45	44	46	28	48	54	42
MAN AND APES HAVE COMMON ANCESTRY								
Yes	46	57	45	39	60	43	40	44
No	47	37	48	52	32	50	52	48
DARWIN'S THEORY OF EVOLUTION PROVEN BY FOSSIL EVIDENCE								
Yes	46	57	48	35	58	43	36	52
No	48	41	44	58	37	47	56	47
HUMAN EVOLUTION								
Belief in evolution	22	25	25	16	30	17	17	28
Belief in creationism	64	60	59	73	52	72	71	56
Belief in intelligent design	10	11	9	9	13	9	8	10

Issuing Rebuke, Judge Rejects Teaching of Intelligent Design

BY LAURIE GOODSTEIN
THE NEW YORK TIMES, DECEMBER 21, 2005

A federal judge ruled on Tuesday that it was unconstitutional for a Pennsylvania school district to present intelligent design as an alternative to evolution in high school biology courses because it is a religious viewpoint that advances "a particular version of Christianity."

In the nation's first case to test the legal merits of intelligent design, the judge, John E. Jones III, issued a broad, stinging rebuke to its advocates and provided strong support for scientists who have fought to bar intelligent design from the science curriculum.

Judge Jones also excoriated members of the Dover, Pa., school board, who he said lied to cover up their religious motives, made a decision of "breathtaking inanity" and "dragged" their community into "this legal maelstrom with its resulting utter waste of monetary and personal resources."

Eleven parents in Dover, a growing suburb about 20 miles south of Harrisburg, sued their school board a year ago after it voted to have teachers read students a brief statement introducing intelligent design in ninth-grade biology class.

The statement said that there were "gaps in the theory" of evolution and that intelligent design was another explanation they should examine.

Judge Jones, a Republican appointed by President Bush, concluded that intelligent design was not science, and that in order to claim that it is, its proponents admit they must change the very definition of science to include supernatural explanations.

Judge Jones said that teaching intelligent design as science in public school violated the First Amendment of the Constitution, which prohibits public officials from using their positions to impose or establish a particular religion.

"To be sure, Darwin's theory of evolution is imperfect," Judge Jones wrote. "However, the fact that a scientific theory cannot yet render an explanation on every point should not be used as a pretext to thrust an untestable alternative hypothesis grounded in religion into the science classroom or to misrepresent well-established scientific propositions."

The six-week trial in Federal District Court in Harrisburg gave intelligent design the most thorough academic and legal airing since the movement's inception about 15 years ago, and was often likened to the momentous Scopes case that put evolution on trial 80 years earlier.

Intelligent design posits that biological life is so complex that it must have been designed by an intelligent source. Its adherents say that they refrain from identifying the designer, and that it could even be aliens or a time traveler.

But Judge Jones said the evidence in the trial proved that intelligent design was "creationism relabeled."

The Supreme Court has already ruled that creationism, which relies on the biblical account of the creation of life, cannot be taught as science in a public school.

Judge Jones's decision is legally binding only for school districts in the middle district of Pennsylvania. It is unlikely to be appealed because the school board members who supported intelligent design were unseated in elections in November and replaced with a slate that opposes the intelligent design policy and said it would abide by the judge's decision.

Lawyers for the plaintiffs said at a news conference in Harrisburg that the judge's decision should serve as a deterrent to other school boards and teachers considering teaching intelligent design.

"It's a carefully reasoned, highly detailed opinion," said Richard Katskee, assistant legal director of Americans United for Separation of Church and State, "that goes through all of the issues that would be raised in any other school district."

Richard Thompson, the lead defense lawyer for the school board, derided the judge for issuing a sweeping judgment in a case that Mr. Thompson said merely involved a "one-minute statement" being read to students. He acknowledged that his side, too, had asked the judge to rule on the scientific merits of intelligent design, but only because it had to respond to the plaintiffs' arguments.

"A thousand opinions by a court that a particular scientific theory is invalid will not make that scientific theory invalid," said Mr. Thompson, the president and chief counsel of the Thomas More Law Center, a public interest firm in Ann Arbor, Mich., that says it promotes Christian values. "It is going to be up to the scientists who are going to continue to do research in their labs that will ultimately determine that."

The scientists who have put intelligent design forward as a valid avenue of scientific research said they were disappointed by Judge Jones's ruling but that they thought its long-term effects would be limited.

"That was a real drag," said Michael J. Behe, a professor of biochemistry at Lehigh University who was the star witness for the intelligent design side. "I think he really went way over what he as a judge is entitled to say."

Dr. Behe added: "He talks about the ground rules of science. What has a judge to do with the ground rules of science? I think he just chose sides and echoed the arguments and just made assertions about our arguments."

William A. Dembski, a mathematician who argues that mathematics can show the presence of design in the development of life, predicted that intelligent design would become much stronger within 5 to 10 years.

Both Dr. Behe and Dr. Dembski are fellows with the Discovery Institute, a leading proponent of intelligent design.

"I think the big lesson is, let's go to work and really develop this theory and not try to win this in the court of public opinion," Dr. Dembski said. "The burden is on us to produce."

Mainstream scientists who have maintained that no controversy exists in the scientific community over evolution were elated by Judge Jones's ruling.

"Jubilation," said Kenneth R. Miller, a professor of biology at Brown University who has actively sparred with intelligent design proponents and testified in the Dover case. "I think the judge nailed it."

Dr. Miller said he was glad that the judge did not just rule narrowly.

Jason D. Rosenhouse, a professor of mathematics at James Madison University in Virginia and a fervent pro-evolution blogger said: "I was laughing as I read it because I don't think a scientist could explain it any better. His logic is flawless, and he hit all of the points that scientists have been making for years."

Before the start of a celebratory news conference in Harrisburg, Tammy Kitzmiller, a parent of two daughters in the Dover district and the named plaintiff in the case, Kitzmiller et al v. Dover, joked with other plaintiffs that she had an idea for a new bumper sticker: "Judge Jones for President."

Christy Rehm, another plaintiff, said to the others, "We've done something amazing here, not only with this decision, but with the election."

Last month, Dover, which usually votes majority Republican, ousted eight school board members who had backed intelligent design and elected the opposition that ran on a Democratic ticket.

Witold Walczak, legal director of the American Civil Liberties Union of Pennsylvania, who helped to argue the case, said, "We sincerely hope that other school districts who may have been thinking about intelligent design will pause, they will read Judge Jones's erudite opinion and they will look at what happened in the Dover community in this battle, pitting neighbor against neighbor."

The judge's ruling said that two of the most outspoken proponents of intelligent design on the Dover school board, William Buckingham and Alan Bonsell, lied in their depositions about how they raised money in a church to buy copies of an intelligent design textbook, "Of Pandas and People," to put in the school library.

Both men, according to testimony, had repeatedly said at school board meetings that they objected to evolution for religious reasons and wanted to see creationism taught on equal footing.

Judge Jones wrote, "It is ironic that several of these individuals, who so staunchly and proudly touted their religious convictions in public, would time and again lie to cover their tracks and disguise the real purpose behind the I.D. policy."

Mr. Bonsell did not respond to a telephone message on Tuesday. Mr. Buckingham, a retired police officer who has moved to Mount Airy, N.C., said, "If the judge called me a liar, then he's a liar."

Mr. Buckingham said he "answered the questions the way they asked them." He called the decision "ludicrous" and said, "I think Judge Jones ought to be ashamed of himself."

The Constitution, he said, does not call for the separation of church and state.

Opponents of intelligent design said Judge Jones's ruling would not put an end to the movement.

In his opinion, Judge Jones traced the history of the intelligent design movement to what he said were its roots in Christian fundamentalism. He seemed especially convinced by the testimony of Barbara Forrest, a historian of science, that the authors of the "Pandas" textbook had removed the word "creationism" from an earlier draft and substituted it with "intelligent design" after the Supreme Court's ruling in 1987.

"We conclude that the religious nature of intelligent design would be readily apparent to an objective observer, adult or child," the judge said. "The writings of leading I.D. proponents reveal that the designer postulated by their argument is the God of Christianity."

Opponents of intelligent design said Judge Jones's ruling would not put an end to the movement, and predicted that intelligent design would take on various guises.

The Kansas Board of Education voted in November to adopt standards that call into question the theory of evolution, but never explicitly mention intelligent design.

Eugenie Scott, executive director, National Center for Science Education, an advocacy group in Oakland, Calif., that promotes teaching evolution, said in an interview, "I predict that another school board down the line will try to bring intelligent design into the curriculum like the Dover group did, and they'll be a lot smarter about concealing their religious intent."

Even after courts ruled against teaching creationism and creation science, Ms. Scott said, "for several years afterward, school districts were still contemplating teaching creation science."

Media Coverage of "Intelligent Design"

By Jason Rosenhouse and Glenn Branch
BioScience, March 2006

Increasingly in the past few years, states and local school districts have had to confront challenges to science education instigated by antievolutionists. Part of the reason for this surge of antievolution activity is the repackaging of creationism in the less overtly religious form of "intelligent design" (ID), which enjoys the support of a number of prominent, politically conservative groups and individuals. As a result of this activity, the news media have produced miles of copy and hours of television footage in their coverage of evolution and ID. The quality of this reporting varies widely, depending on the media outlet.

Terms of the Debate

The landscape of this debate has changed considerably since the antievolution flare-ups of the 1970s and 1980s. Terms such as "creation science" and "originally created kinds" have nearly disappeared from the discussion. Defenders of a young Earth and ancient global flood are still around, but a string of adverse court decisions made it impossible for them to have their ideas openly presented in public school science classes.

Proponents of ID often bristle at the term "creationism." In the public consciousness, that term is laden with the sort of religious connotations ID supporters wish to abjure. They claim that there are scientifically rigorous methods by which the products of an intelligent agent can be identified, independent of any knowledge concerning the history of those products. As an elementary illustration, they point to the faces on Mount Rushmore: Only the action of an intelligent agent, and not natural forces like weathering and erosion, can account for them. It is in large part this assertion of scientific rigor that ID proponents claim distinguishes their creed from traditional creationism. In making this assertion, however, they ignore the fact that the creation scientists before them made similar claims of scientific rigor.

Proponents of ID further claim that their methods, when applied to biological systems such as the human blood clotting cascade, reveal that these complex systems must be the products of an intelligent agent. It is natural to suppose that the designer is God, but ID proponents, mindful of potential constitutional challenges to teaching that idea in the public schools, are adamant that science is incapable of validating that identification.

Most ID literature is devoted to attacks on modern evolutionary theory. Proponents claim that the scientific lines of evidence used to support evolution are dubious at best. Such arguments are recognizable as a proper subset of the traditional creationist canon. Also prominent in ID-generated literature are philosophical and sociological claims that likewise have precursors in creation science. Among these claims are that modern science unreasonably and arbitrarily bars supernatural explanations from receiving a fair hearing, and that "the Darwinian establishment" is so powerful and monolithic that the traditional venues of scientific discourse are closed to ID proponents.

It is not the purpose of this article to analyze the merits of ID arguments. The major scientific and philosophical claims for ID have already been assessed and refuted in several books (Miller 1999, Pennock 1999, 2001, Young and Edis 2004). The religious motivations of the ID movement, along with its attempts to craft a constitutionally acceptable form of creationism, have also been documented at book length (Forrest and Gross 2004). Nor is it our intention either to argue, as Forrest and Gross (2004) and Coyne (2005) have, that ID is a historical continuation of traditional creationism, or to pursue a sociological investigation of the antievolution movement (such as Eve and Harrold 1991 or Toumey 1994).

Rather, our intention is to consider the manner in which the nation's major media outlets cover the evolution–ID issue. Writing in *Columbia Journalism Review*, Chris Mooney and Matthew Nisbet (2005) note that in covering this issue, the media transforms "an entirely lopsided debate within the scientific community" into an "evenly divided one in the popular arena." We agree with this conclusion, and will present concrete examples of the rhetorical techniques through which this transformation is achieved. On the basis of these examples, we will offer several suggestions for how scientists can more fruitfully engage the media.

News about the evolution–ID issue seems to break almost daily. Consequently, any analysis of media coverage will be outdated almost as soon as it is written. In this article we focus exclusively on a half year's worth of media—articles written and shows aired between November 2004 and April 2005. We begin with coverage in the wake of the presidential election, because the ID movement received a boost with the reelection of President George W. Bush, who, as he publicly disclosed during a press conference in August 2005, is sympathetic to the ID cause. For a discussion of more recent examples of media coverage, we recommend the article by Mooney and Nisbet (2005). Furthermore, we have confined our analysis to just three forms of media: major national newspapers, weekly newsmagazines, and cable television news channels.

Newspapers

Several themes emerge in the news coverage of evolution–creationism disputes in the largest newspapers in the United States. First, very little science finds its way into the coverage. Because most of these disputes concern public education, it is usually a reporter who specializes in education or politics, rather than a science reporter, who is assigned to the story. Evolution is often not defined at all, or is defined in grossly inaccurate terms. The history of evolutionary theory typically is given short shrift as well. Evolution is often described as "Charles Darwin's theory of evolution" (as if biology has not progressed since 1859). This usage persists for at least two reasons: the media's need to put a human face on the issue by attaching a name to the theory, and the creationists' sustained campaign to present evolution as a relic of the 19th century. Thus, evolution supporters are "Darwinists," and anything related to modern evolutionary science is "Darwinism."

The journalistic need for succinct definitions also distorts the treatment of young-Earth creationism and ID. The reporter typically makes a clear distinction between the two, which has the effect of making ID seem like a science-based critique of evolution, not a religion-based attack on it. A typical example comes from the article "'Call to Arms' on Evolution," published in *USA Today*:

> To most scientists, evolution is defined as changes in genes that lead to the development of species. They see it as a fundamental insight in biology.
>
> Creationism is the belief that species have divine origin.
>
> Another alternative to evolution is called "intelligent design." Proponents believe some cellular structures are too complex to have evolved over time. (Vergano and Toppo 2005, p. 7D)

None of these definitions would be regarded as adequate by any of the participants in the debate. Even worse, they present a distorted picture in which ID is distinct from creationism and both are "alternatives" to evolution, and in which the massive evidence for evolution, on the one hand, and the scientific bankruptcy and religious agendas of the "alternatives," on the other, are completely neglected. Also typical is a back-and-forth style of reporting, in which a quote from one side is mechanically balanced in the next paragraph by a quote from the other. There is little attempt to evaluate the merits of what each side is saying. The *USA Today* article quoted above supplies a good example:

> Says Stephen Meyer of the Seattle-based Discovery Institute, which promotes intelligent design: "My first reaction is we're seeing evidence of some panic among the official spokesmen for science." He says [NAS President Bruce] Alberts is wrong— that intelligent design is not creationism but a scientific

approach more openminded than Charles Darwin's theory of evolution.

Biologists retort that any reproducible data validating intelligent design would be welcome in science journals. "If there were indeed deep flaws in parts of evolutionary biology, then scientists would be the first to charge in there," says Jeffrey Palmer of Indiana University in Bloomington.

Meyer counters that scientific leaders such as Alberts block a fair hearing of evolution alternatives. "There are powerful institutional and systematic conventions in science that keep (intelligent) design from being considered a scientific process," he says. (Vergano and Toppo 2005, p. 7D)

From such exchanges a lay reader could hardly avoid drawing the erroneous conclusion that there is some genuine controversy here between rival scientific camps. But it is a conclusion that a more intrepid reporter could have forestalled, for example, by asking the editors of scientific journals whether ID proponents are in fact submitting any papers purportedly providing evidence for ID.

Although most news articles on this subject take a skeptical, but polite, stance toward ID, they are also quick to point out the obvious political and religious aspects of the dispute. The growth in popularity of ID is typically, and correctly, linked to the general resurgence of religious fundamentalism in the United States. A cogent example comes from the article "Battle on Teaching Evolution Sharpens" from the *Washington Post* (Slevin 2005). The article opens as follows: "Propelled by a polished strategy crafted by activists on America's political right, a battle is intensifying across the nation over how students are taught about the origins of life. Policymakers in 19 states are weighing proposals that question the science of evolution" (Slevin 2005, p. A1).

Later, we come to this: "They are acting now because they feel emboldened by the country's conservative currents and by President Bush, who angered many scientists and teachers by declaring that the jury is still out on evolution. Sharing strong convictions, deep pockets and impressive political credentials—if not always the same goals—the activists are building a sizable network" (Slevin 2005, p. A1).

The *Post* article thus does an unusually good job of making it clear that antievolution advocacy has more to do with political strategizing than with scientific truth.

Newsmagazines

Even though magazine reporters typically have more time and more resources to devote to their stories, reporters who specialize in politics or education are usually the ones who write them. So you will still find the polite, but skeptical, tone toward ID, the "dueling quotations" approach to journalism, and a regrettable tendency to frame the debate in the preferred terms of the ID side. A recent example comes from *Newsweek*. The title and subtitle set the tone: "Doubting Darwin: How Did Life, in Its Infinite Complexity, Come to Be? A Controversial New Theory Called 'Intelligent Design' Asserts a Supernatural Agent Was at Work." The article lays out its version of the debate in the second paragraph:

> Eighty years after the Scopes trial, in which a Tennessee high-school teacher was convicted of violating a state law against teaching evolution, Americans are still fighting the slur that they share an ancestry with apes. This time, though, the battle is being waged under a new banner—not the Book of Genesis, but "intelligent design," a critique of evolution couched in the language of science. . . . Proponents of I.D., clustered around a Seattle think tank called the Discovery Institute, regard it as an overdue challenge to Darwinism's monopoly over scientific discourse. (Adler 2005, pp. 45–46)

Notice the references to "Darwinism" and "Darwinians." Notice also the implication that ID is based on science and not religion. Later in the paragraph, a lawyer for the ACLU offers the standard counterargument that ID relies on the supernatural, and hence is unscientific. While that is indeed a major shortcoming, the utter failure of ID to produce anything of scientific interest is not mentioned. These are the standard tropes for the major newsmagazines no less than for the daily newspapers.

Time magazine's foray into this genre came in its 31 January 2005 issue. It sets the familiar tone in its opening paragraphs:

> The intellectual underpinnings of the latest assault on Darwin's theory come not from Bible-wielding Fundamentalists but from well-funded think tanks promoting a theory they call intelligent design, or I.D. for short. Their basic argument is that the origin of life, the diversity of species and even the structure of organs like the eye are so bewilderingly complex that they can only be the handiwork of a higher intelligence (name and nature unspecified). (Lemonick 2005, pp. 53–54)

More than *Newsweek*'s article, however, the one in *Time* makes an attempt to grapple with the fringe nature of ID: "But many scientists—and science teachers—don't think there is any valid criticism. Sure, some 350 scientists have signed a declaration challenging *evolution*. [Emphasis added, to draw attention to the reporter's unwitting adoption of a device employed by the Discovery Institute, whose "A Scientific Dissent from Darwinism" refers just to "Darwin's theory of evolution" and "random mutation and natural selection," but then is billed and construed as a challenge to *evolution*.] But many tens of thousands of scientists reject I.D.'s core argument—that evolution can't produce complex structures" (Lemonick 2005, p. 54).

And while the reporter engages in the aforementioned back-and-forth quotation pattern, he also offers a critical evaluation:

> Then there's the assertion that evolution is "just" a theory. "They are playing on the public's lack of understanding of what a scientific theory is," says Bingman. "It's more than a guess. It's a set of hypotheses that has been tested over time." Evolutionary theory does have gaps, but so do relativity, quantum theory and the theory of plate tectonics. West says those are different because scientists in these fields, unlike evolutionists, aren't afraid of intellectual debate. Evolutionists counter that they have welcomed challenges. (Lemonick 2005, p. 54)

He rather drops the ball in the next sentence, though: "They developed the theory of punctuated equilibriums, for example, to address the fact that species remain unchanged for long periods, then suddenly start evolving."

With explanations like this, which manage to combine a mischaracterization of punctuated equilibria with a misleading suggestion of its origin, it is hardly surprising that people do not understand the basics of evolutionary theory.

Television

Coverage of the evolution–creationism dispute on the broadcast television networks (ABC, CBS, NBC, and PBS) is similar to that provided by the print media, although because of the limitations of the medium, oversimplification is even more prevalent. It is on the cable news stations that something quite different, and far more distressing, appears.

All three of the major cable news networks (CNN, MSNBC, and Fox) devote a major portion of their prime-time lineups to debate-oriented shows. Such debate as takes place is invariably superficial. This is especially evident in their handling of evolution–creationism disputes, where it is simply taken for granted that evolution is an all-encompassing, atheistic worldview. Far from being a modest attempt to unravel the major events of natural history after life appeared, cable news treats evolution as an attempt to explain the origins of life, the Earth, or even the universe, and to deny the existence of God and promote immoral behavior in the bargain.

One example comes from the 21 April 2005 edition of the MSNBC show *Hardball*, for which host Chris Matthews's guests were the Reverend Terry Fox of Wichita, Kansas, and Eugenie C. Scott of the National Center for Science Education. At one point, Matthews persisted in interrogating Scott, an agnostic, about her personal religious beliefs—"Do you believe that everything we live—do you think our lives, who we are, the world around us, was an accident of some explosion millions of years ago and it led to everything we see? Do you believe it was all just natural selection or just an accident of scientific development?"—despite her repeated insistence that what is at issue is what ought to be taught in science classes.

An examination of the transcript reveals a second major theme of cable news discussion of this issue: Time is not allotted equally to both sides. The segment comprised just under 1600 words. Matthews himself claimed the bulk of this verbiage, with roughly 700 words. Fox came in second with 560, with Scott having just 329 words. The result is the superficial impression that the creationist is winning the debate.

The highest-rated of these cable shows is Fox's *The O'Reilly Factor*. In its excursion into the evolution–creationism fray on 18 January 2005, host Bill O'Reilly introduced the segment this way:

> Spurred on by the ACLU and other so-called freedom groups, a nationwide controversy has erupted over teaching intelligent design in public school biology classes. Intelligent design is the belief that a higher power created the universe. Some Americans want it taught alongside evolution. In the Dover, Pennsylvania, school district, teachers wouldn't even mention intelligent design, so today the district superintendent had to do it. Lawsuits are flying.

These are political shows, and the people who host them have no scientific credentials—in discussing scientific issues, they frequently reveal their ignorance. Furthermore, they tend to be biased toward the religious right and thus sympathetic to ID and hostile to evolution. These shortcomings are clearly on display in O'Reilly's introduction. Note the gratuitous slap at the ACLU and the benign definition of ID (if ID were really just the idea that a higher power created the universe, then it would be perfectly consistent with evolution).

O'Reilly's guest that night was biologist Michael Grant. Consider the following exchange:

> O'REILLY: OK. But science is incomplete in this area of creationism, is it not?
>
> GRANT: Science is always incomplete in all areas.
>
> O'REILLY: Well, I don't agree with that. Science is not always incomplete, and I'll give you an example. There are 24 hours in a day. All right. That's science. And there are four seasons. That's science. So you can state things with certainty in biology or any other science you want. However, if I'm a student in your class and you're telling me, well, there might have been a meteor or big bang, or there might have been this or there might have been that, I'm going to raise my hand like the wise guy I am and say, "Professor, might there be a higher power that contributed to the fact that we're all here?" And you say— what?

GRANT: I say that's something you need to discuss with other people. You need to do that in the proper class. In the biology class we deal with science, with the natural world and what fits our conventional concepts of science.

O'REILLY: But, what if it turns out there is a God and He did create the universe and you die and then you figure that out? Aren't you going to feel bad that you didn't address that in your biology class?

GRANT: Well, to quote a famous quote . . .

O'REILLY: Because then it would be science, wouldn't it? You know, if tomorrow the deity came down and proved himself, then it would be science, wouldn't it, sir?

Again, the host seized most of the time for himself. But obviously O'Reilly is confused about key scientific issues. His examples of scientific certainty are actually mere matters of convention ("season" in meteorology; "day" in the sense of "mean solar day" in astronomy). And anything short of certainty—"there might have been a meteor or big bang, or there might have been this or there might have been that"—he regards as a pretext for invoking divine intervention. Moreover, it is clear that in O'Reilly's view, evolution is an inherently atheistic theory.

Reading the transcript does not tell the full story, however. Grant, no doubt flummoxed by the rapid-fire hostility of O'Reilly's questions, looked a bit dazed and unsure of himself. O'Reilly, by contrast, was supremely confident. On television, flash and style count for far more than substance.

At least Matthews and O'Reilly had actual scientists on the show. By contrast, on the 15 December 2004 edition of the MSNBC show *Scarborough Country*, guest host Pat Buchanan introduced the following panel to discuss the relative merits of evolution and creationism: "Joining me now, Dr. Al Mohler, president of the Southern Baptist Theological Seminary; David Silverman, a spokesman for American Atheists; Christian music artist Natalie Grant And Republican strategist Jack Burkman is still with us." Not one panel member had any scientific credentials.

Given the prearranged harmony of the panelists—save for the foil from American Atheists—it is not surprising that the discussion contained fawning exchanges like this one:

BUCHANAN: I want to go back to you, Al Mohler, and the point I was talking to Dave Silverman about. It seems to me if, in the public schools you teach Darwinism, the theory of evolution, and no other alternative, and since Darwinism points to no God, what you are doing then is indoctrinating children in the belief that there is no God and no creator. And it seems to me that crosses the line of separation of church and state or a violation of the First Amendment every bit as much as the charges in the

Scopes trial.

MOHLER: Well, that's absolutely right. And, Mr. Buchanan, you know the US Supreme Court has ruled that secular humanism is itself a religion. And Darwinism, in terms of its theory, in terms of the way it's taught, in terms of its structure, it's undeniably a religious truth claim. It's just the religion in which there is no God or, as others would say, there's nothing left for God to do. It is an inherently anti-Christian religion. But it is a religion. And that's why they're holding to their dogma so tenaciously and that's why they're so scared to death and paranoid, insecure about the rise of intelligent design. It scares them to death.

This is what cable news viewers are being told about the nature of science generally and evolution in particular; the print media do little better. What is the scientific community going to do about it?

Conclusions

We have only scratched the surface of this topic. Regional newspapers vary widely in their coverage of, and respect for, evolution. Partisan magazines, especially conservative ones, have a great many things to say on the subject Television coverage on the major networks is substantially more sedate than it is on cable. And the extent and quality of coverage of these issues is influenced by a host of journalistic, social, political, economic, and religious factors too numerous and too broad to discuss thoroughly in this article. But, even on the basis of such a limited and preliminary discussion, there are clear morals to extract for the scientific community.

Antievolutionists have a very attractive message to market. They do not tell journalists that they want a certain myopic religious viewpoint presented as legitimate science. Instead, they talk about presenting both sides, being open-minded, opposing censorship, and presenting all the evidence. The only way for the evolutionist to counteract this is to show that creationism's scientific pretensions are nonsense. That is precisely what cannot be done in a brief newspaper article or television appearance.

Scientists therefore need to become more savvy in their dealings with the media. Toward that end, we offer the following suggestions.

In any encounter between scientists and the media on the subject of creationism, declare first and foremost that the specific scientific assertions of ID proponents are false. State unambiguously that evolutionary theory is perfectly capable in principle of explaining the formation of complex biological systems, and, indeed, has done so in practice many times.

Avoid arguing simply that ID is unscientific because of its reliance on the supernatural, or that present-day mysteries may eventually yield to scientific explanations. Both of these assertions are certainly correct, but they play into the hands of ID proponents. The former fosters the impression, which ID proponents are keen to convey, that defenders of evolution are merely ruling ID unscientific by definitional fiat, while the latter seems to concede that there are vast explanatory holes in modern evolutionary theory.

Invest time in preparation. Read the books and articles produced by young-Earth creationists and ID proponents. Scientifically knowledgeable readers may find this a frustrating and aggravating experience, but it has to be done in order to respond. Also read material on the historical, religious, philosophical, educational, and legal issues associated with the dispute (a good starting place is Scott 2005).

Watch your language, with respect to both terminology and tone. Don't assume that your readers and listeners understand that a theory is more than a hunch or a guess, for example. Similarly, speak of *accepting* rather than *believing in* evolution, since the latter will strike many as expressing a statement of faith rather than a judgment based on the evidence. As for tone, the manner in which you deliver your message can be as important as the content of your message. Try to sound calm, informed, and knowledgeable—especially in public appearances and on radio or television.

Expect the religion card to be played. Creationists—abetted by a handful of scientists, to be sure—have convinced a large segment of the public that evolution is intrinsically atheistic. Whether or not you are religious yourself, be prepared to point out that evolution is accepted simply on the basis of the overwhelming evidence in its favor by scientists of all faiths, and that quite a few religious denominations have made their theological peace with evolution.

Be ready, too, to rebut the inevitable appeal to fairness. Perhaps the most powerful argument in the creationist repertoire is the idea of giving students "both views" and leaving it up to them to decide. What is truly unfair, of course, is to cheat students of an adequate science education by telling them anything other than the truth: Evolution is at the core of modern biology.

Look for opportunities to become a spokesperson. You might begin small, by submitting letters to the editor of your local newspapers applauding, criticizing, or expanding on recent articles on evolution–creationism issues. More ambitiously, inquire about the possibility of submitting an op-ed piece supporting evolution education. You can ask your university press office to list you as an expert on the topic. You can also cultivate reporters on your own: Drop a friendly note to reporters who write on evolution–creationism issues, commenting on their stories and offering your help when they next do a story on the topic.

With the rise of blogs (short for "Web log") as cheap but influential media sources, consider speaking out on the Internet. Among the scientists who use blogs as platforms to defend the teaching of evolution are P. Z. Myers (University of Minnesota at Morris; *http://scienceblogs.com/pharyngula*), John M. Lynch (Arizona State University; *http://scienceblogs.com/strangerfruit*), and the first author of this essay (*http://evolutionblog.blogspot.com/*). Such blogging can have profound effects. For example, when an article arguing for ID was published, under suspicious circumstances, in a legitimate scientific journal, a detailed critique quickly appeared on the collaborative blog The Panda's Thumb (*www.pandasthumb.org*, to which Myers, Lynch, and the first author contribute). This critique was subsequently cited in news stories in *The Scientist* and *Nature*.

For most scientists, it is natural to be circumspect when discussing complex scientific issues. That approach is totally ineffective in dealing with the media. What seems like sober reflection in an academic setting comes off as weakness when printed in a newspaper or stated on television. Proponents of ID are effective precisely because they spend so much time thinking about public relations. Scientists need to do likewise.

Anticipating a storm of controversy over *On the Origin of Species*, Thomas Henry Huxley wrote, "I am sharpening up my beak and claws in readiness." Scientists today, too, should be taking themselves to the grindstone.

References cited

Adler J. 2005. Doubting Darwin. Newsweek, 7 February, pp. 44–50.

Coyne JA. 2005. The faith that dares not speak its name: The case against intelligent design. The New Republic, 22 August, pp. 21–33.

Eve RA, Harrold FB. 1991. The Creationist Movement in Modern America. Boston: Twayne.

Forrest B, Gross PR. 2004. Creationism's Trojan Horse: The Wedge of Intelligent Design. New York: Oxford University Press.

Lemonick M. 2005. Stealth attack on evolution. Time, 31 January, pp. 53-54.

Miller KR. 1999. Finding Darwin's God: A Scientist's Search for Common Ground between God and Evolution. New York: Cliff Street Books.

Mooney C, Nisbet MC. 2005. Undoing Darwin. Columbia Journalism Review. September–October, pp. 30–39.

Pennock RT. 1999. Tower of Babel: The Evidence against the New Creationism. Cambridge (MA): MIT Press.

———, ed. 2001. Intelligent Design Creationism and Its Critics: Philosophical, Theological, and Scientific Perspectives. Cambridge (MA):MIT Press.

Scott EC. 2005. Evolution vs. Creationism: An Introduction. Berkeley (CA): University of California Press.

Slevin P. 2005. Battle on teaching evolution sharpens. Washington Post, 14 March, p. Al.

Toumey CP. 1994. God's Own Scientists: Creationists in a Secular World. New Brunswick (NJ): Rutgers University Press.

Vergano D, Toppo G. 2005. "Call to arms" on evolution. USA Today, 23 March, p. 7D.

Young M, Edis T, eds. 2004. Why Intelligent Design Fails: A Scientific Critique of the New Creationism. New Brunswick (NJ): Rutgers University Press.

The Descent of the Straw Man

By Denis Boyles
National Review Online, November 30, 2005

The evolution debate seems made for liberals. It casts them as thoughtful and open-minded thinkers and conservatives as zealots and simpletons—or at least that's how it looks through the media prism. It doesn't matter how many times you remind people, as Jonah Goldberg once memorably did, "Your Darwin fish are safe," the Left will still seize on the caricatures of that debate to pillory whatever other conservative initiatives are around, drowning out the rest of the conversation. It's hard to argue the virtues of a complex issue such as school choice, for example, while all the shouting is about what a lousy science book the Bible makes.

It's a trick as old as Scopes's monkey. The famous 1925 Darrow-Bryan trial was a set-up, remember, an invention of the ACLU, who wanted to challenge a Tennessee law. So they found a willing "victim" in a part-time biology teacher in Dayton, a small town that volunteered to provide the venue for the famous monkey trial—until it became clear that the press was happy to make Dayton into the monkey. The case established a winning strategy forever after. It's astonishing that conservatives still rise to the bait instead of taking the initiative to reform public education altogether.

Nevertheless, that's what happened in Dover, Pennsylvania, and what's happening now in Kansas. The evolution controversy has dominated the news here for months. Despite the fact that nothing the state Board of Education has done with its standards will change in the slightest what happens in Kansas schoolrooms, the ongoing controversy is giving a solid boost to the state's "moderate" Republicans and Democrats on a wide range of issues, none of which have anything to do with evolution. The Left believes no other issue has the potential to turn this red state blue, which is why it rages on. It's allowed the secularists to demean the religiously inclined with impunity—but also laid bare the thoughts of those who viciously revile those who hold those beliefs. The evolution debate makes anyone who touches it look terrible.

To find out how terrible, just go to Lawrence, home of the University of Kansas, one of the two areas in the state to vote for Kerry over Bush. Wading into the evolution controversy, the university has announced "courses"—really, '60s-style teach-ins—designed to do nothing but ridicule the religious Right, each taught by a prof with an agenda.

Personally, I think it's a good thing that universities are finally being used for satire rather than self-parody, and on this point I appear to agree with the chairman of KU's religious-studies department, Paul Mirecki, and the campus group he mentors, the 120-member "Society of Open-minded Atheists and Agnostics"—a.k.a. SOMA.

Mirecki announced plans earlier this month to teach "the fundies"—as he referred to his theological enemies—a lesson by offering a course called "Intelligent Design, Creationism and other Religious Mythologies." The course announcement was instantly picked up by AP, CNN, and a bunch of daily papers and TV stations across the country. "The KU faculty has had enough," Mirecki told reporters with gusto.

Personally, I think it's a good thing that universities are finally being used for satire rather than self-parody.

Conservatives were irate, of course, but universities—well, what can you do? The class would have passed into the archive of goofy courses all colleges offer for whatever reason. However, Mirecki had made the strategic error of using SOMA's Yahoo usergroup to post his view that the purpose of the course was not education. It was theater: "To my fellow damned," he wrote to the students, "Its [sic] true, the fundies have been wanting to get I.D. and creationism into the Kansas public schools, so I thought 'why don't I do it?' I will teach the class with several other lefty KU professors . . . The fundies want it all taught in a science class, but this will be a nice slap in their big fat face . . . I expect it will draw much media attention. The university public relations office will have a press release on it in a few weeks, I also have contacts at several regional newspapers.

The forum post was forwarded to an ad-hoc group of conservative Kansas bloggers and writers led by John Altevogt, a former Kansas City Star columnist and a political activist. Altevogt blew the whistle and the embarrassing post caused KU chancellor Bob Hemenway—a fervent backer of the course—to blink. Calling voters "fundies" wasn't helpful to a public university.

After nearly a week of backpedaling, Mirecki apologized for the statement: "I have always practiced my belief that there is no place for impertinence and name calling in a serious academic class," he wrote. "My words in the email do not represent my teaching philosophy or the style I use in class." The word "Mythologies" was dropped from the description. The chancellor said he would conducting a "review" of Mirecki's e-mail. The university insisted the show would go on.

But the cat was out of the bag. As Hemenway was telling reporters the course was "serious," Mirecki was telling readers of his SOMA list—at least until a few days ago apparently open to any who

wished to join and read it—"This thing will be a hoot." Conservatives had set about conducting a review of their own, sorting
through and circulating the rest of Mirecki's SOMA posts on the
Internet, and they came away more concerned than ever. "These
aren't just lighthearted messages," said Altevogt.

Mirecki seemed to enjoy adolescent outrageousness as much as
the students. In one note, for example, a SOMA member suggests
creating anti-Gideon pamphlets: While the Gideons are distribut-
ing their propaganda, we would distribute a single folded page of
the same height and width of a Gideon bible. The cover would contain wording on the order of "For complete assurance that your
soul will be safe from the Fires of Hell . . . " The inside would continue 'quit believing that FUCKING God and Jesus BULLSHIT.—
Join us, the Society of Open Minded Atheist and Agnostics. "Our
Bible is a quicker read." Mirecki's response: "I think the language
is a bit strong in what you suggest, but I still like the general
idea . . ." and went on to offer his own version. In another, Mirecki
explained to students that German Christians saw "Nazism as
compatible (the fulfillment of?) Christianity [sic], with Hitler as
final messiah."

In a post he published to the list last May, he wrote, "I had my
first Catholic 'holy communion' when I was a kid in Chicago and
when I took the bread-wafer the first time, it stuck to the roof of
my mouth, and as I was secretly trying to pry it off with my tongue
as I was walking back to my pew with white clothes and with my
hands folded, all I could think was that it was Jesus' skin, and I
started to puke, but I sucked it in and drank my own puke. That's
a big part of the Catholic experience. I don't think most Catholics
really know what they are supposed to believe, they just go home
and use condoms and some of them beat their wives and hus-
bands." Mirecki went on to explain that he was going to meet with
Monsignor Vince Krische, then at the university's Catholic Center.

What did Msgr. Krische remember about the meeting? Not much.
Although Mirecki claimed in his posts that the two were "very good
friends," Msgr. Krische tells me the two had met only twice, once at
the Catholic Center and once at dinner. The priest could offer no
explanation for the comments. "I just don't know why he would say
such a thing. I think this is a very offensive and irresponsible thing
for him to say. What is it based on? Why would he say this?"
Mirecki did not return a call asking for comment and clarification.

Maybe Mirecki didn't understand how false the sense of privacy
on the Internet is, or maybe it was meant to be a joke, although for
Altevogt and many other conservatives, the controversy is no
laughing matter. "Our concerns," Altevogt tells me, "are simple
and not related to one particular course, but to more general
issues. First, we're worried about the academic decline of the university under [Chancellor] Hemenway: KU has slipped seven
places during his tenure and things like this may be one reason
why. Second, we are concerned when an entire category of people—

including the very students he is most likely to run into in his current assignment as an instructor teaching classes about religion—is maligned by the faculty sponsor of a university-sanctioned organization." And third, Altevogt says, is a concern for the religious studies department itself, which, he said, has become "a hotbed of religious bigotry and intolerance."

State Sen. Karin Brownlee says Mirecki's SOMA comments were "consistent with the tone and attitude of his other remarks" concerning the course he wants to teach. "I think students look up to a professor, whether he's an adviser or in a classroom . . . but as the head of a religion department he clearly has a disdain for those who have a Christian belief."

When asked to comment on Mirecki's comments regarding Catholics, a spokesman for the university simply directed me to a web posting of Mirecki's apology for his previous remarks against Protestants.

Ask Ken Lay or Duke Cunningham why smart people do not-smart things. As a thoughtful scholar—as opposed to his new career as a polemicist—Mirecki has made valuable and important contributions to his field. Why the co-author of The Gospel of the Savior would indulge in witless Catholic-bashing—not to mention those poor Gideons!—seems mysterious, especially considering the collateral damage.

> *As a thoughtful scholar—as opposed to his new career as a polemicist—Mirecki has made valuable and important contributions to his field.*

Altevogt and others, including some members of the legislature—the source of the university's funding—are now concerned that even in red-state Kansas the university is so disconnected from the people who pay for it that somebody so apparently "lacking in respect [for religion]," as Brownlee put it, has been given charge of KU's department of religious studies. As Altevogt notes, asking a man who believes—or is at least willing to casually write on a listserv germane to his profession—that Catholics "beat their wives" to run the religious-studies department has the feel of asking David Duke to oversee the African-American studies department.

Religious conservatives say they hope both Mirecki and Hemenway will retreat to doing what they were hired to do and leave political theater to the drama department. But the religious-studies department may not be the healthiest environment for any kind of retreat: "The majority of my colleagues here in the dept[ment] are agnostics or atheists, or they just don't care," Mirecki wrote in explaining, correctly, that it wasn't the job of the department to make converts. "If any of [the other professors] are theists, it hasn't been obvious to me in the 15 years I've been here."

"Amen," Altevogt says.

Intelligent Design?

EDITED BY RICHARD MILNER AND VITTORIO MAESTRO
NATURAL HISTORY, APRIL 2002

The idea that an organism's complexity is evidence for the existence of a cosmic designer was advanced centuries before Charles Darwin was born. Its best-known exponent was English theologian William Paley, creator of the famous watchmaker analogy. If we find a pocket watch in a field, Paley wrote in 1802, we immediately infer that it was produced not by natural processes acting blindly but by a designing human intellect. Likewise, he reasoned, the natural world contains abundant evidence of a supernatural creator. The argument from design, as it is known, prevailed as an explanation of the natural world until the publication of the Origin of Species in 1859. The weight of the evidence that Darwin had patiently gathered swiftly convinced scientists that evolution by natural selection better explained life's complexity and diversity. "I cannot possibly believe" wrote Darwin in 1868, "that a false theory would explain so many classes of facts."

In some circles, however, opposition to the concept of evolution has persisted to the present. The argument from design has recently been revived by a number of academics with scientific credentials, who maintain that their version of the idea (unlike Paley's) is soundly supported by both microbiology and mathematics. These antievolutionists differ from fundamentalist creationists in that they accept that some species do change (but not much) and that Earth is much more than 6,000 years old. Like their predecessors, however, they reject the idea that evolution accounts for the array of species we see today, and they seek to have their concept—known as intelligent design—included in the science curriculum of schools.

Most biologists have concluded that the proponents of intelligent design display either ignorance or deliberate misrepresentation of evolutionary science. Yet their proposals are getting a hearing in some political and educational circles and are currently the subject of a debate within the Ohio Board of Education. Although Natural History does not fully present and analyze the intelligent-design phenomenon in the pages that follow, we offer, for the reader's information, brief position statements by three leading proponents of the theory, along with three responses. The section concludes with an overview of the intelligent-design movement by a philosopher and cultural historian who has monitored its history for more than a decade.

The Challenge of Irreducible Complexity

By MICHAEL J. BEHE

Every living cell contains many ultrasophisticated molecular machines.

Scientists use the term "black box" for a system whose inner workings are unknown. To Charles Darwin and his contemporaries, the living cell was a black box because its fundamental mechanisms were completely obscure. We now know that, far from being formed from a kind of simple, uniform protoplasm (as many nineteenth-century scientists believed), every living cell contains many ultrasophisticated molecular machines.

Irreducibly complex systems appear very unlikely to be produced by numerous, successive, slight modifications of prior systems.

How can we decide whether Darwinian natural selection can account for the amazing complexity that exists at the molecular level? Darwin himself set the standard when he acknowledged, "If it could be demonstrated that any complex organ existed which could not possibly have been formed by numerous, successive, slight modifications, my theory would absolutely break down."

Some systems seem very difficult to form by such successive modifications—I call them irreducibly complex. An everyday example of an irreducibly complex system is the humble mousetrap. It consists of (1) a flat wooden platform or base; (2) a metal hammer, which crushes the mouse; (3) a spring with extended ends to power the hammer; (4) a catch that releases the spring; and (5) a metal bar that connects to the catch and holds the hammer back. You can't catch a mouse with just a platform, then add a spring and catch a few more mice, then add a holding bar and catch a few more. All the pieces have to be in place before you catch any mice.

Irreducibly complex systems appear very unlikely to be produced by numerous, successive, slight modifications of prior systems, because any precursor that was missing a crucial part could not function. Natural selection can only choose among systems that are already working, so the existence in nature of irreducibly complex biological systems poses a powerful challenge to Darwinian theory. We frequently observe such systems in cell organelles, in which the removal of one element would cause the whole system to cease functioning. The flagella of bacteria are a good example. They are outboard motors that bacterial cells can use for self-propulsion. They have a long, whiplike propeller that is rotated by a molecular motor. The propeller is attached to the motor by a universal joint. The motor is held in place by proteins that act as a stator. Other proteins act as bushing material to allow the driveshaft to penetrate the bacterial membrane. Dozens of different kinds of proteins are necessary for a working flagellum. In the absence of almost any of them, the flagellum does not work or cannot even be built by the cell.

Another example of irreducible complexity is the system that allows proteins to reach the appropriate subcellular compartments. In the eukaryotic cell there are a number of places where specialized tasks, such as digestion of nutrients and excretion of wastes, take place. Proteins are synthesized outside these compartments and can reach their proper destinations only with the help of "signal" chemicals that turn other reactions on and off at the appropriate times. This constant, regulated traffic flow in the cell comprises another remarkably complex, irreducible system. All parts must function in synchrony or the system breaks down. Still another example is the exquisitely coordinated mechanism that causes blood to clot.

Biochemistry textbooks and journal articles describe the workings of some of the many living molecular machines within our cells, but they offer very little information about how these systems supposedly evolved by natural selection. Many scientists frankly admit their bewilderment about how they may have originated, but refuse to entertain the obvious hypothesis: that perhaps molecular machines appear to look designed because they really are designed.

I am hopeful that the scientific community will eventually admit the possibility of intelligent design, even if that acceptance is discreet and muted. My reason for optimism is the advance of science itself, which almost every day uncovers new intricacies in nature, fresh reasons for recognizing the design inherent in life and the universe.

The Flaw in the Mousetrap
BY KENNETH R. MILLER

Intelligent design fails the biochemistry test.

To understand why the scientific community has been unimpressed by attempts to resurrect the so-called argument from design, one need look no further than Michael J. Behe's own essay. He argues that complex biochemical systems could not possibly have been produced by evolution because they possess a quality he calls irreducible complexity. Just like mousetraps, these systems cannot function unless each of their parts is in place. Since "natural selection can only choose among systems that are already working," there is no way that Darwinian mechanisms could have fashioned the complex systems found in living cells. And if such systems could not have evolved, they must have been designed. That is the totality of the biochemical "evidence" for intelligent design.

Ironically, Behe's own example, the mousetrap, shows what's wrong with this idea. Take away two parts (the catch and the metal bar), and you may not have a mousetrap but you do have a three-part machine that makes a fully functional tie clip or paper clip. Take away the spring, and you have a two-part key chain. The catch of some mousetraps could be used as a fishhook, and the wooden base as a paper-weight; useful applications of other parts include everything from toothpicks to nutcrackers and clipboard holders. The point, which science has long understood, is that bits and pieces of supposedly irreducibly complex machines may have different—but still useful—functions.

> *Bits and pieces of supposedly irreducibly complex machines may have different—but still useful—functions.*

Behe's contention that each and every piece of a machine, mechanical or biochemical, must be assembled in its final form before anything useful can emerge is just plain wrong. Evolution produces complex biochemical machines by copying, modifying, and combining proteins previously used for other functions. Looking for examples? The systems in Behe's essay will do just fine.

He writes that in the absence of "almost any" of its parts, the bacterial flagellum "does not work." But guess what? A small group of proteins from the flagellum does work without the rest of the machine—it's used by many bacteria as a device for injecting poisons into other cells. Although the function performed by this small part when working alone is different, it nonetheless can be favored by natural selection.

The key proteins that clot blood fit this pattern, too. They're actually modified versions of proteins used in the digestive system. The elegant work of Russell Doolittle has shown how evolution duplicated, retargeted, and modified these proteins to produce the vertebrate blood-clotting system.

And Behe may throw up his hands and say that he cannot imagine how the components that move proteins between subcellular compartments could have evolved, but scientists actually working on such systems completely disagree. In a 1998 article in the journal Cell, a group led by James Rothman, of the Sloan-Kettering Institute, described the remarkable simplicity and uniformity of these mechanisms. They also noted that these mechanisms "suggest in a natural way how the many and diverse compartments in eukaryotic cells could have evolved in the first place." Working researchers, it seems, see something very different from what Behe sees in these systems—they see evolution.

If Behe wishes to suggest that the intricacies of nature, life, and the universe reveal a world of meaning and purpose consistent with a divine intelligence, his point is philosophical, not scientific. It is a philosophical point of view, incidentally, that I share. However, to support that view, one should not find it necessary to pretend that we know less than we really do about the evolution of living systems. In the final analysis, the biochemical hypothesis of intelligent design fails not because the scientific community is closed to it but rather for the most basic of reasons—because it is overwhelmingly contradicted by the scientific evidence.

Detecting Design in the Natural Sciences
BY WILLIAM A. DEMBSKI

Intelligence leaves behind a characteristic signature.

In ordinary life, explanations that invoke chance, necessity, or design cover every eventuality. Nevertheless, in the natural sciences one of these modes of explanation is considered superfluous—namely, design. From the perspective of the natural sciences, design, as the action of an intelligent agent, is not a fundamental creative force in nature. Rather, blind natural causes, characterized by chance and necessity and ruled by unbroken laws, are thought sufficient to do all nature's creating. Darwin's theory is a case in point.

But how do we know that nature requires no help from a designing intelligence? Certainly, in special sciences ranging from forensics to archaeology to SETI (the Search for Extraterrestrial Intelligence), appeal to a designing intelligence is indispensable. What's more, within these sciences there are well-developed techniques for identifying intelligence. Essential to all these techniques is the ability to eliminate chance and necessity.

For instance, how do the radio astronomers in Contact (the Jodie Foster movie based on Carl Sagan's novel of the same name) infer the presence of extraterrestrial intelligence in the beeps and pauses they monitor from space? The researchers run signals through computers that are programmed to recognize many preset patterns. Signals that do not match any of the patterns pass through the "sieve" and are classified as random. After years of receiving apparently meaningless "random" signals, the researchers discover a pattern of beats and pauses that corresponds to the sequence of all the prime numbers between 2 and 101. (Prime numbers, of course, are those that are divisible only by themselves and by one.) When a sequence begins with 2 beats, then a pause, 3 beats, then a pause . . . and continues all the way to 101 beats, the researchers must infer the presence of an extraterrestrial intelligence.

Here's why. There's nothing in the laws of physics that requires radio signals to take one form or another. The sequence is therefore contingent rather than necessary. Also, it is a long sequence and therefore complex. Note that if the sequence lacked complexity, it could easily have happened by chance. Finally, it was not just complex but also exhibited an independently given pattern or specification (it was not just any old sequence of numbers but a mathematically significant one—the prime numbers).

Intelligence leaves behind a characteristic trademark or signature—what I call "specified complexity." An event exhibits specified complexity if it is contingent and therefore not necessary; if it is complex and therefore not easily repeatable by chance; and if it is specified in the sense of exhibiting an independently given pattern. Note that complexity in the sense of improbability is not sufficient to eliminate chance: flip a coin long enough, and you'll witness a highly complex or improbable event. Even so, you'll have no reason not to attribute it to chance.

The important thing about specifications is that they be objectively given and not just imposed on events after the fact. For instance, if an archer shoots arrows into a wall and we then paint bull's-eyes around them, we impose a pattern after the fact. On the other hand, if the targets are set up in advance ("specified") and then the archer hits them accurately, we know it was by design.

Intelligence leaves behind a characteristic trademark or signature—what I call "specified complexity."

In my book The Design Inference, I argue that specified complexity reliably detects design. In that book, however, I focus largely on examples from the human rather than the natural sciences. The main criticism of that work to date concerns whether the Darwinian mechanism of natural selection and random variation is not in fact fully capable of generating specified complexity. More recently, in No Free Lunch, I show that undirected natural processes like the Darwinian mechanism are incapable of generating the specified complexity that exists in biological organisms. It follows that chance and necessity are insufficient for the natural sciences and that the natural sciences need to leave room for design.

Mystery Science Theater
By ROBERT T. PENNOCK

The case of the secret agent

William A. Dembski claims to detect "specified complexity" in living things and argues that it is proof that species have been designed by an intelligent agent. One flaw in his argument is that he wants to define intelligent design negatively, as anything that is not chance or necessity. But the definition is rigged: necessity, chance, and design are not mutually exclusive categories, nor do they exhaust the possibilities. Thus, one cannot detect an intelligent agent by the process of elimination he suggests. Science requires positive evidence. This is so even when attempting to detect the imprint of human intelligence, but it is especially true when assessing the extraordinary claim that biological complexity is intentionally designed.

In this regard, Dembski's archery and SETI analogies are red herrings, for they tacitly depend on prior understanding of human intellect and motivation, as well as of relevant causal processes. A design inference like that in the movie Contact, for instance, would rely on background knowledge about the nature of radio signals and other natural processes, together with the assumption that a sequence of prime numbers is the kind of pattern another scientist might choose to send as a signal. But the odd sequences found within DNA are quite unlike a series of prime numbers. Dembski has no way to show that the genetic patterns are "set up in advance" or "independently given."

Dembski has been promoted as "the Isaac Newton of information theory," and in his writings, which include the books he cites in the essay here, he insists that his "law of conservation of information"

In the evolutionary process, an increase in biological complexity does not represent a "free lunch."

---

proves that natural processes cannot increase biological complexity. He doesn't lay out his case here, and a refutation would require too much space. Suffice it to say that a connection exists between the technical notion of information and that of entropy, so Dembski's argument boils down to a recasting of an old creationist claim that evolution violates the second law of thermodynamics. Put simply, this law states that in the universe, there is a tendency for complexity to decrease. How then, ask the creationists, can evolutionary processes produce more complex life-forms from more primitive ones? But we have long known why this type of argument fails: the second law applies only to closed systems, and biological systems are not closed.

In the evolutionary process, an increase in biological complexity does not represent a "free lunch"—it is bought and paid for, because random genetic variation is subjected to natural selection by the environment, which itself is already structured. In fact, researchers are beginning to use Darwinian processes, implemented in computers or in vitro, to evolve complex systems and to provide solutions to design problems in ways that are beyond the power of mere intelligent agents.

If we really thought that genetic information was like the signal in Contact, shouldn't we infer we were designed by extraterrestrials? Intelligent-design theorists do sometimes mention extraterrestrials as possible suspects, but most seem to have their eyes on a designer more highly placed in the heavens. The problem is, science requires a specific model that can be tested. What exactly did the designer do, and when did he do it? Dembski's nebulous hypothesis of design, even if restricted to natural processes, provides precious little that is testable, and once supernatural processes are wedged in, it loses any chance of testability.

Newton found himself stymied by the complex orbits of the planets. He could not think of a natural way to fully account for their order and concluded that God must nudge the planets into place to make the system work. (So perhaps in this one sense, Dembski is the Newton of information theory.) The origin of species once seemed equally mysterious, but Darwin followed the clues given in nature to solve that mystery. One may, of course, retain religious faith in a designer who transcends natural processes, but there is no way to dust for his fingerprints.

Elusive Icons of Evolution
BY JONATHAN WELLS

What do Darwin's finches and the four-winged fruit fly really tell us?

Charles Darwin wrote in 1860 that "there seems to be no more design in the variability of organic beings and in the action of natural selection, than in the course which the wind blows." Although many features of living things appear to be designed, Darwin's theory was that they are actually the result of undirected processes such as natural selection and random variation.

Scientific theories, however, must fit the evidence. Two examples of the evidence for Darwin's theory of evolution—so widely used that I have called them "icons of evolution"—are Darwin's finches and the four-winged fruit fly. Yet both of these, it seems to me, show that Darwin's theory cannot account for all features of living things.

Darwin's finches consist of several species on the Galápagos Islands that differ mainly in the size and shape of their beaks. Beak differences are correlated with what the birds eat, suggesting that the various species might have descended from a common ancestor by adapting to different foods through natural selection. In the 1970s, biologists Peter and Rosemary Grant went to the Galápagos to observe this process in the wild.

In 1977 the Grants watched as a severe drought wiped out 85 percent of a particular species on one island. The survivors had, on average, slightly larger beaks that enabled them to crack the tough seeds that had endured the drought. This was natural selection in action. The Grants estimated that twenty such episodes could increase average beak size enough to produce a new species.

When the rains returned, however, average beak size returned to normal. Ever since, beak size has oscillated around a mean as the food supply has fluctuated with the climate. There has been no net change, and no new species have emerged. In fact, the opposite may be happening, as several species of Galápagos finches now appear to be merging through hybridization.

Darwin's finches and many other organisms provide evidence that natural selection can modify existing features—but only within established species. Breeders of domestic plants and animals have been doing the same thing with artificial selection for centuries. But where is the evidence that selection produces new features in new species?

New features require new variations. In the modern version of Darwin's theory, these come from DNA mutations. Most DNA mutations are harmful and are thus eliminated by natural selection. A few, however, are advantageous—such as mutations that increase antibiotic resistance in bacteria and pesticide resistance in plants and animals. Antibiotic and pesticide resistance are often cited as evidence that DNA mutations provide the raw materials for evolution, but they affect only chemical processes. Major evolutionary changes would require mutations that produce advantageous anatomical changes as well.

Alongside Darwin's argument against design, students should also be taught that design remains a possibility.

Normal fruit flies have two wings and two "balancers"—tiny structures behind the wings that help stabilize the insect in flight. In the 1970s, geneticists discovered that a combination of three mutations in a single gene produces flies in which the balancers develop into normal-looking wings. The resulting four-winged fruit fly is sometimes used to illustrate how mutations can produce the sorts of anatomical changes that Darwin's theory needs.

But the extra wings are not new structures, only duplications of existing ones. Furthermore, the extra wings lack muscles and are therefore worse than useless. The four-winged fruit fly is severely handicapped—like a small plane with extra wings dangling from its tail. As is the case with all other anatomical mutations studied so far, those in the four-winged fruit fly cannot provide raw materials for evolution.

In the absence of evidence that natural selection and random variations can account for the apparently designed features of living things, the entire question of design must be reopened. Alongside Darwin's argument against design, students should also be taught that design remains a possibility.

The Nature of Change
By EUGENIE C. SCOTT

Evolutionary mechanisms give rise to basic structural differences.

Without defining "design," Wells asserts that "many features of living things appear to be designed." Then he contrasts natural selection (undirected) with design (directed), apparently attempting to return to the pre-Darwinian notion that a Designer is directly responsible for the fit of organisms to their environments. Darwin proposed a scientific rather than a religious explanation: the fit between organisms and environments is the result of natural selection. Like all scientific explanations, his relies on natural causation.

> *Evolutionary theory is not inadequate. It fits the evidence just fine.*

Wells contends that "Darwin's theory cannot account for all features of living things," but then, it doesn't have to. Today scientists explain features of living things by invoking not only natural selection but also additional biological processes that Darwin didn't know about, including gene transfer, symbiosis, chromosomal rearrangement, and the action of regulator genes. Contrary to what Wells maintains, evolutionary theory is not inadequate. It fits the evidence just fine.

Reading Wells, one might not realize the importance of the Grants' careful studies, which demonstrated natural selection in real time. That the drought conditions abated before biologists witnessed the emergence of new species is hardly relevant; beak size does oscillate in the short term, but given a long-term trend in climate change, a major change in average size can be expected. Wells also overstates the importance of finch hybridization: it is extremely rare, and it might even be contributing to new speciation. The Galápagos finches remain a marvelous example of the principle of adaptive radiation. The various species, which differ morphologically, occupy different adaptive niches. Darwin's explanation was that they all evolved from a common ancestral species, and modern genetic analysis provides confirming evidence.

Wells admits that natural selection can operate on a population and correctly looks to genetics to account for the kind of variation that can lead to "new features in new species." But he contends that mutations such as those that yield four-winged fruit files do not produce the sorts of anatomical changes needed for major evolutionary change. Can't he see past the example to the principle? That the first demonstration of a powerful genetic mechanism happened to be a nonflying fly is irrelevant. Edward Lewis shared a Nobel Prize for the discovery of the role of these genes, known as the Ubx complex. They are of extraordinary importance because genes of this type help explain body plans—the basic structural differences between a mollusk and a mosquito, a sponge and a spider.

Ubx genes are among the HOX genes, found in animals as different as sponges, fruit flies, and mammals. They turn on or off the genes involved in—among other things—body segmentation and the production of appendages such as antennae, legs, and wings. What specifically gets built depends on other, downstream genes. The diverse body plans of arthropods (insects, crustaceans, arachnids) are variations on segmentation and appendage themes, variations that appear to be the result of changes in HOX genes. Recent research shows that fly Ubx genes suppress leg formation in abdominal segments but that crustacean Ubx genes don't; a very small Ubx change results in a big difference in body plan.

Mutations in these primary on/off switches are involved in such phenomena as the loss of legs in snakes, the change from lobe fins to hands, and the origin of jaws in vertebrates. HOX-initiated segment duplication allows for anatomical experimentation, and natural selection winnows the result. "Evo Devo"—the study of evolution and development—is a hot new biological research area, but Wells implies that all it has produced is crippled fruit flies.

Wells argues that natural explanations are inadequate and, thus, that "students should also be taught that design remains a possibility." Because in his logic, design implies a Designer, he is in effect recommending that science allow for nonnatural causation. We actually do have solid natural explanations to work with, but even if we didn't, science only has tools for explaining things in terms of natural causation. That's what Darwin did, and that's what we're trying to do today.

The Newest Evolution of Creationism
By BARBARA FORREST

Intelligent design is about politics and religion, not science.

The infamous August 1999 decision by the Kansas Board of Education to delete references to evolution from Kansas science standards was heavily influenced by advocates of intelligent-design theory. Although William A. Dembski, one of the movement's leading figures, asserts that "the empirical detectability of intelligent causes renders intelligent design a fully scientific theory," its proponents invest most of their efforts in swaying politicians and the public, not the scientific community.

Launched by Phillip E. Johnson's book Darwin on Trial (1991), the intelligent-design movement crystallized in 1996 as the Center for the Renewal of Science and Culture (CRSC), sponsored by the Discovery Institute, a conservative Seattle think tank. Johnson, a law professor whose religious conversion catalyzed his antievolution efforts, assembled a group of supporters who promote design theory through their writings, financed by CRSC fellowships. According to an early mission statement, the CRSC seeks "nothing less than the overthrow of materialism and its damning cultural legacies."

Johnson refers to the CRSC members and their strategy as the Wedge, analogous to a wedge that splits a log—meaning that intelligent design will liberate science from the grip of "atheistic naturalism." Ten years of Wedge history reveal its most salient features: Wedge scientists have no empirical research program and, consequently, have published no data in peer-reviewed journals (or elsewhere) to support their intelligent-design claims. But they do have an aggressive public relations program, which includes conferences that they or their supporters organize, popular books and articles, recruitment of students through university lectures sponsored by campus ministries, and cultivation of alliances with conservative Christians and influential political figures.

The Wedge aims to "renew" American culture by grounding society's major institutions, especially education, in evangelical religion. In 1996, Johnson declared: "This isn't really, and never has been, a debate about science. It's about religion and philosophy." According to Dembski, intelligent design "is just the Logos of John's Gospel restated in the idiom of information theory." Wedge strategists seek to unify Christians through a shared belief in "mere" creation, aiming—in Dembski's words—"at defeating naturalism and its consequences." This enables intelligent-design proponents to coexist in a big tent with other creationists who explicitly base their beliefs on a literal interpretation of Genesis.

"As Christians," writes Dembski, "we know naturalism is false. Nature is not self-sufficient. . . . Nonetheless neither theology nor philosophy can answer the evidential question whether God's interaction with the world is empirically detectable. To answer this question we must look to science." Jonathan Wells, a biologist, and Michael J. Behe, a biochemist, seem just the CRSC fellows to give intelligent design the ticket to credibility. Yet neither has actually done research to test the theory, much less produced data that challenges the massive evidence accumulated by biologists, geologists, and other evolutionary scientists. Wells, influenced in part by Unification Church leader Sun Myung Moon, earned Ph.D.'s in religious studies and biology specifically "to devote my life to destroying Darwinism." Behe sees the relevant question as whether "science can make room for religion." At heart, proponents of intelligent design are not motivated to improve science but to transform it into a theistic enterprise that supports religious faith.

Wedge supporters are at present trying to insert intelligent design into Ohio public-school science standards through state legislation. Earlier the CRSC advertised its science education site by assuring teachers that its "Web curriculum can be appropriated without textbook adoption wars"—in effect encouraging teachers to do an end run around standard procedures. Anticipating a test case, the Wedge published in the Utah Law Review a legal strategy for winning judicial sanction. Recently the group almost succeeded in inserting into the federal No Child Left Behind Act of 2001 a "sense of the Senate" that supported the teaching of intelligent design. So the movement is advancing, but its tactics are no substitute for real science.

III. The Genetic Blueprint

Editors' Introduction

The complete human genome—often referred to as the "blueprint" of life— is contained within 23 pairs of chromosomes, which (with few exceptions) reside in every cell in the human body. Beginning in 1990, scientists from around the world began contributing to the immense undertaking of mapping all of the 3 billion chemical base pairs that make up human DNA. Those findings, available on publicly accessible databases, may not only aid scientists in the development of medicines but might also help to resolve some of the questions about the history of human evolution that paleontologists have been unable to answer using the fossil record alone. By comparing the DNA of two species, scientists can determine approximately when they diverged, providing a clearer, more accurate picture of the tree of life.

As Douglas J. Futuyma explains in "On Darwin's Shoulders," although evolution was widely accepted within the scientific community only 20 years after the publication of *On the Origin of Species*, it has taken a century for the scientific community to understand the mechanism behind the process. Even after the scientific community had accepted Mendel's notion that heredity was the result of one generation passing along discrete particles (now called genes) to the next, researchers had to wait for the advent of high-speed computers and the development of more advanced lab techniques before they could begin to catalog and analyze the genetic codes of various species.

Thomas Hayden reports in "All in the Family" that scientists at the American Museum of Natural History are using a network of hundreds of computers to try to construct the first comprehensive "tree of life"—a diagram that would indicate the relationships among the 1.5 million or so known species. When Darwin roughly sketched such a diagram, he had only a pen, paper, and the physical characteristics of various species with which to work. Now, by tapping into a computer network of information, scientists can quickly analyze large amounts of genetic data, creating a far more accurate picture of our family tree.

At the base of this tree should exist what scientists refer to as the last universal common ancestor, or LUCA, a primitive cell that lived millions of years ago and from which all species on earth later diverged. LUCA would not have left a fossil record, as Garry Hamilton explains in "Mother Superior," but by comparing the genes of numerous forms of life, researchers are attempting to create a rough sketch of what that creature was like. In the process, they have come across some controversial findings that suggest that DNA may have evolved on two separate occasions.

In "Evo Devo," Gareth Cook explains how scientists in the field of evolutionary development biology are trying to explain how the great diversity among the earth's species arose. Though humans share 98 percent of their genetic code with chimpanzees, subtle distinctions in the way these genes are expressed create significant differences. Minute changes in an organism's genetic code during its embryonic development can result in dramatic alterations in the physiology of an animal, which in turn can become an advantage (or disadvantage) in terms of natural selection.

Another recent and controversial study is covered by Gareth Cook in the final article of this chapter, "Humans, Chimps May Have Bred After Split." Researches at the Massachusetts Institute of Technology used genetic data to estimate when human ancestors first diverged from chimpanzees and came up with a date that was much later than the one suggested by the fossil record. Consequently, the scientists concluded that the two species must have interbred. Paleontologists greeted this announcement with skepticism, but researchers are in the process of collecting additional primate DNA to conduct a more thorough analysis.

On Darwin's Shoulders

By Douglas J. Futuyma
Natural History, November 2005

Charles Darwin's daring proposal that all living things have descended with modification from "a few forms or one" gained wide acceptance among biologists within twenty years of its publication in the Origin of Species. That vision of common ancestry revolutionized studies in comparative anatomy, comparative embryology, and taxonomy, and has become the unifying principle of all biology. But Darwin's seminal notion of natural selection—his truly original insight about the primary mechanism of evolution—was received more cautiously, and remains contentious among some biologists to this day.

Natural selection can preserve variations only if they are heritable, but Darwin (and his younger colleague, the naturalist Alfred Russel Wallace) had formulated the theory before anyone understood how heredity works. The missing piece of the puzzle turned out to be the discovery by the Austrian priest and botanist Gregor Mendel—published in 1865 but not appreciated until 1900—that heredity depends on the transmission of discrete particles, now called genes. By 1910 biologists recognized that genes can mutate at random into different forms, known as alleles. Joining the principles of genetics with Darwin's theory of natural selection initiated a second great episode of progress in evolutionary biology. Today the field is in the midst of a third flowering, and the pace of discovery and understanding is accelerating in realms that neither Darwin nor Wallace could have imagined.

The tale of Darwin's own intellectual journey into uncharted waters has reached mythical proportions, but the story of the second great episode deserves a brief retelling, because it bears on how biological science is conducted today. In the 1930s and 1940s, experimental geneticists, mathematical theorists, paleontologists, and systematists together forged the evolutionary synthesis, also known as the modern synthesis or synthetic theory of evolution. Among other things, they noted that when new alleles first arise, by mutation, they are very rare in a population. Some disappear right away, because they lead to the death of the individual carriers. Many are simply inconsequential—they do not even change the proteins for which they code—and do not affect the survival and reproduction of the organism. Their frequency changes merely at random, a process known as genetic drift. A minority of them may increase by chance and become typical of the species.

On occasion, alleles, often acting in combination, enhance the survival or reproduction of their carriers, and therefore increase in frequency within a population through the process of natural selection. Although natural selection can act in other ways, purifying or preserving older alleles in the population, the architects of the evolutionary synthesis emphasized its role in driving an increase in the frequency of new alleles that had arisen by mutation. The results are increasingly well-honed adaptations—those features of organisms that, as Darwin said, "so justly excite our admiration.

The scientists who forged the evolutionary synthesis agreed that speciation often occurs when various populations of a species become separated by mountains, rivers, unsuitable habitat, or other geophysical barriers. Genetic changed can then spread within the various population fragments without transferring from one fragment to another. An accumulation of such genetic changes would render the fragments incapable of interbreeding, through some behavioral or genetic incompatibility.

At that point they are considered different species. As time passes, these species, together with their various descendant species, continue to diverge. Proponents of the evolutionary synthesis, then, followed Darwin in envisioning macroevolution—speciation and evolution in the long term—as a gradual, incremental process.

Evolutionary research in the 1950s and 1960s was directed largely at testing the principles of the evolutionary synthesis. Biologists who focused on so-called microevolutionary changes—observable, short-term genetic processes within small populations—generally confirmed its validity. One of the most important accomplishments of this period was the proof that most characters are genetically variable within a population. Thus, when environments change, adaptation often proceeds rapidly without new mutations, because alleles that prove to be advantageous are already present in the population.

The third and current episode of progress in evolutionary biology was launched in the late 1960s, when two new technologies exploded on the scene. One was the ready availability of powerful computers and information processors. For biologists, this technology opened the door to compiling and analyzing databases of ever greater size and complexity, in ways that had previously been impractical or even impossible. The second new technology was biomolecular analysis, first applied to determining the sequences of amino acids that make up certain proteins, such as hemoglobins. Today that technology has blossomed into a sophisticated array of methods for sequencing DNA and, in general, for studying how genes work.

One key application of computers has been to analyze the phylogenetic relations between organisms—"family trees"—showing which species are more closely and which more distantly related. Before the computer, such family trees were based on relatively few details of anatomy, which often were insufficient for firm conclusions about relationships. High-speed computing enabled biologists to analyze many more characters of the various species, including DNA and protein sequences, which are often easier to interpret than anatomical features.

When relationships among many species are analyzed, the number of possible family trees that must be evaluated is huge. Computers also made it possible to compare them with one another and to determine the most parsimonious, or least tortuous, way of mapping the interspecies relations. The analysis of similarities and differences at the molecular level confirmed some traditional ideas about relations among various species, but it also brought surprises. For example, protein comparisons showed that humans share an immediate common ancestor with chimpanzees and gorillas. It had been thought previously that humans were equally related to all the great apes.

With the ability to determine amino-acid sequences, it was also natural to ask, how many differences are there between corresponding sequences of two related species, and how do those counts compare with paleontologists' estimates of how long ago the two lineages diverged? When the data were plotted, they suggested, surprisingly, that the rate of molecular evolution is roughly constant. Evolutionary biologists knew that the rate of evolution of anatomical features varies greatly from time to time and species to species, and so they had assumed that proteins would conform to the same pattern.

To account for the constancy, the Japanese population geneticist Motoo Kimura proposed his "neutral theory of molecular evolution." According to the theory, many changes in the genome are caused by genetic drift rather than by natural selection, and simply have no effect on the organism. Genetic drift operates at about the same rate all the time, unlike natural selection, which drives changes mostly when environments change. Kimura's hypothesis has stood up to nearly three decades of testing, and it has become an important addition to the evolutionary synthesis, which minimized the importance of genetic drift.

At about the same time Kimura developed his theory, the geneticists Richard C. Lewontin and John L. Hubby, both then at the University of Chicago, tested certain proteins for uniformity within a species. Using a technique called protein electrophoresis to examine proteins in the fruit fly Drosophila pseudoobscura, they discovered that about a third of them displayed differing genetic variants. That was far more variation than anyone had expected. Moreover, other investigators found similar levels of variation in almost every other species they examined, including humans.

Were the variations neutral ones, of the kind suggested by Kimura, or were they maintained by natural selection, perhaps as adaptations to variations within a species' environment? The current evidence suggests that both explanations apply, but their relative importance remains uncertain.

The variations themselves have proved useful as genetic markers, helping answer questions that previously had been intractable: To what extent are geographically separate populations of a species also separate genetically? Do closely related species differ by few or many genes? Do genes "leak" between related species?

In the 1990s protein-based studies were largely replaced by analyses of the sequence of base pairs, the building blocks that make up DNA. Such analyses were made possible by another technological breakthrough, the polymerase chain reaction (PCR), invented in 1983 by Kary Mullis. From one or a few DNA molecules, PCR gives rise to huge numbers of copies, which are necessary to obtain the sequence of base pairs. The technique provides DNA data for studies of phylogenetic relationships among species and for investigating natural selection and genetic drift within species. DNA sequences of entire genomes—from microorganisms of many kinds and from people, mice, and a growing number of animal and plant species—are making it possible for geneticists to study the effects of natural selection and genetic drift on thousands of genes and to trace the origins of new kinds of genes with novel functions.

> *To what extent are geographically separate populations of a species also separate genetically?*

Perhaps the most exciting new field made possible by the new molecular technologies is evolutionary developmental biology ("evo-devo"). Its focus is to explore how the pathways of embryonic development evolve and give rise to major changes in adult morphology. For example, geneticists now know that certain genes, including those called Hox genes, regulate the activity of other genes. The Hox genes can cause some structures to repeat themselves, creating multiple segments, legs, or vertebrae.

Some research in evo-devo is leading to a moderate reevaluation of traditional ideas. For example, according to the prevailing view, morphological and other features of the organism evolve by a slow accumulation of slight incremental changes. But some studies have shown that just a few gene differences, each with disproportionately large effects, can cause major differences in the characteristics of closely related species. Darwin's principle of gradual change still holds overall, but not all change is as gradual as biologists used to think.

Among the most important questions still being addressed in studies of evolution is how speciation takes place. In particular, what gives rise to reproductive isolation among populations of a single species? Many biologists, following Darwin's lead, have assumed that divergence into separate species is brought about as natural selection acts on reproductive traits. Until recently, though, there have been precious few data to clarify how or why that may happen.

Most species differ from each other in characteristics that adapt them to somewhat different habitats, food, and other environmental factors. One hypothesis is that reproductive isolation, leading to speciation, is precipitated by characteristics that are simply adaptations to distinct environments. For example, Daniel J. Funk, a biologist at Vanderbilt University in Nashville, Tennessee, and Patrik Nosil, a graduate student in biosciences at Simon Fraser University in Burnaby, British Columbia, tested that hypothesis in studies of leaf beetles and stick insects. They observed how much interbreeding took place between geographically distinct populations. They found that if two such populations were adapted to different species of host plants, the insect populations were less likely to interbreed than if they were adapted to the same plant species. The finding is consistent with the idea that speciation can be a side effect of specialized ecological adaptation.

Sexual selection is thought to be more intense in polygamous than monogamous species.

An alternative proposal is that species can arise because of sexual selection, a particular kind of natural selection. Female preference for males with certain features can cause males with even more exaggerated features to be more reproductively successful. If females from distinct populations prefer males that display slightly different characters, such as coloration, the differences between the two groups may become increasingly exaggerated, until the males of one group cease to have any sex appeal to the females of the other.

Sexual selection is thought to be more intense in polygamous than monogamous species. In one study, the diversity of species was compared among several pairs of "sister clades" of birds—lineages that share an immediate common ancestor. Shaibal Mitra, a graduate student in evolutionary biology at the University of Chicago at the time the work was done, and his colleagues found that a clade of polygamous species, such as birds of paradise, usually has diversified into more species than its monogamous sister clade, such as the crowlike manucode birds. The pattern strongly suggests that sexual selection contributes to the origin of species.

Various knotty problems continue to puzzle evolutionary biologists. Why, for instance, do so many species reproduce sexually rather than asexually? Most sexually reproducing species produce roughly equal numbers of sons and daughters, and so only half those progeny (the female half) produce babies. In contrast, all the offspring of an asexual female are baby-producing females. Other things being equal, the second means of reproduction should quickly dominate. Because that does not happen, there must be a powerful compensating advantage to sexual reproduction. There are even some species, such as whiptail lizards, whose populations include both sexual and asexual types of females, yet the asexual type does not seem to come to dominate the population.

Sexual reproduction does provide a species with adaptive flexibility, because it is constantly giving rise to new combinations of genes. Thus sex may help prevent or forestall extinction if a species environment changes. As one might expect, species with very old asexual lineages are rare. But natural selection has no foresight. It cannot be expected to provide a species with a feature that acts only as an insurance policy against some future contingency. Darwinian natural selection operates on differences between individuals of a species in features that affect individual reproduction or survival.

Plenty of advantages to sexual reproduction have been proposed. One is that the shuffling of genes in a sexual species can separate harmful mutant genes from advantageous genes, enabling natural selection to purge the harmful ones more efficiently. Another is that defective genes are often repaired during sexual reproduction. And a third is that sexual females may produce more variable offspring, which can live and reproduce themselves in a greater variety of circumstances, so that on average, sexual females may leave more surviving offspring.

The more one learns about evolutionary mechanisms, the more questions one can pose. How could alternative gene splicing have evolved, whereby a single gene encodes two or more different proteins? What prevents transposable DNA sequences, which can multiply within the genome and infest it like weeds in a garden, from taking over the genome? How do plant and animal species manage to survive, despite the high rate at which bacterial and viral parasites can evolve and overcome their hosts' defenses? Are there general rules that can explain why some groups (beetles, flowering plants) have diversified go much more than others (scorpionflies, cycads)?

Delve into almost any subject, no matter how specialized and arcane, and you will find biologists working on unanswered questions, and usually arguing with others about the likely answers. As science presses beyond the limits of the known and the understood into the unknown and the enigmatic, such disagreements reveal not that the science is faulty, but rather that it is alive and well.

All in the Family

By Thomas Hayden
U.S. News & World Report, June 3, 2002

Visiting a natural history museum can be a little like attending a Broadway play; the highly polished show is the main attraction, but much of the real magic happens backstage. At the American Museum of Natural History in New York, going "backstage" means taking a trip down to the basement in a clunky freight elevator. Just beyond the carpentry workshop, in a chilled, darkened room, lurks Circe, a network of 560 desktop computers tied together with a medusa's mane of red cables. Homer's mythical enchantress was a weaver, and so is her namesake. At blinding speeds, this "cluster computer" is weaving data about living things into a fabric of relationships—a family tree of life.

When Charles Darwin published The Origin of Species in 1859, the tree of life was the only illustration he used. It was a rough sketch—a statement of principle, more than anything else—showing organisms branching outward as their descendants evolved into new species. Aided by a flood of genetic data and powerful computers, biologists can finally contemplate finishing Darwin's sketch. This week at the AMNH, his intellectual descendants will meet to launch a coordinated effort to assemble a universal tree of life.

It may take years or decades of collecting specimens and analyzing data. But even a partial tree will be a powerful tool. "Virtually everything we do in biology is comparative," says Joel Cracraft, AMNH's curator of birds. "You can't understand an organism without comparing it to others along the tree." It will also aid medical scientists, who will pick over the tree for clues to how diseases emerged and where cures might be found. For the rest of us, the tree already offers lessons in humility, such as humans' close kinship to the fishes and the surprising status of mushrooms, closer to us than they are to potatoes.

No sooner had Adam risen from the biblical dust than he started naming the animals; classifying nature seems to be a basic human instinct. These days the effort is called phylogeny, and it is not just an exercise in naming. Its goal is to trace evolutionary relationships, by cataloging and comparing the characters—DNA sequences, the shapes of ankle bones or seed pods—that hint at which organisms are close relatives and which have long been separated. It's like a planetwide game of "one of these things is not like the others": You put the monkeys and rabbits on one branch, the bananas and carrots on another, and pretty soon you've got the rudiments of a phylogenetic tree, or tree of life.

As scientists have learned new ways to play this game, the shape of the tree has changed, sometimes dramatically. Until about 1990, most biologists pictured a tree with five major branches: animals, plants, and fungi at the top, protozoa and bacteria at the bottom. Then University of Illinois microbiologist Carl Woese announced that a comparison of the vital molecules that cells use to copy DNA and make proteins pointed to a very different tree, with three roughly equal trunks, or domains, emerging from an ancient root.

Bacteria (think *E. coli*) occupy one trunk; the Eucarya—pond scum, people, and everything in between—occupy another. A third belongs to the Archaea, exotic microbes that were once lumped with bacteria but, as Woese showed, are actually a distinct domain of life, more closely related to the Eucarya. As different as people and hydrogen-eating microbes seem, "Archaea and Eucarya have the same basic tool set," says Sandra Baldauf, a University of York biologist charged with the daunting task of giving a rough outline of the universal tree at the AMNH meeting.

Climbing the Branches

Molecules let Woese identify the major trunks of the tree, but specialists trying to map its luxuriant branches have found that molecules are not always enough. In the 1970s, molecular biologists were confident that they would soon work out the true tree based on differences in genetic sequences. But different genes evolve in different ways, so they often tell conflicting stories about how organisms are related. "You can't just pick a few organisms and a few genes and say, 'Here's my crazy tree,'" says Dan Janies, an AMNH researcher who along with arthropod curator Ward Wheeler developed Circe.

Physical characters, such as anatomical features and cellular structure, have their own problems. Collecting and measuring specimens is time-consuming. Appearances can deceive tree builders, as when "convergent evolution" makes lookalikes out of species that actually parted ways millions of years ago, like whales and fish or birds and bats. And in the vast domains of Bacteria and Archaea, microbes have precious little anatomy to compare.

The tree still looks scraggly, with only some 50,000 of the 1.5 million or so known species in place, but researchers think they now have the tools and know-how to fill it out. Different lines of evidence often result in contradictory trees. But when scientists analyze all the evidence—DNA, cellular structure, anatomy, and even behavior, such as nest building or seed dispersal—and include both living and fossil relatives, the data tell a more consistent tale. "Every character is part of the same story, even if they tell different versions," says Janies.

Using this "total evidence" approach, biologists are now building a convincing account of who begot whom, and they are turning up some unlikely relatives. Arrange the birds, crocodiles, and mammals on a tree, for example, and birds and mammals look like sister groups. "But if you put in the dinosaurs," says Wheeler, "you see the birds, crocs, and dinos on one side with the mammals far away

> *"We are all fish."*—Harry Greene, Cornell University herpetologist

on the other." Similar analyses, based on DNA and newly unearthed fossils, suggest that whales evolved from land animals that looked an awful lot like mangy dogs and are close cousins to the hippopotamus. "Whales are so different from other mammals that it wasn't clear where they fit," says Maureen O'Leary, an evolutionary biologist at the State University of New York–Stony Brook.

Just a few minutes tracing the existing tree is enough to shatter preconceptions. Fungi are more closely related to animals than to plants, and reptiles have more in common with mammals than with amphibians. Starfish are closer to mammals than they are to shellfish. And speaking of fish—not that oysters and starfish really are fish—Cornell University herpetologist Harry Greene has news that may unsettle those already disturbed at the thought that our ancestors were apes. In fact, says Greene, all animals with four limbs, including you, your mother, and your ape ancestors, belong to a branch of the fish lineage. "We are all fish."

Building a universal tree has practical uses, too. Scientists often try to puzzle out what a newly discovered gene does by comparing it with similar genes in other organisms—and they can sharpen those guesses if they know how closely related those organisms are. Fine branches of the tree describing how pathogens are related can help epidemiologists track the emergence and spread of diseases. And ecologists trying to predict the impact of an invasive species can often glean clues from its closest relatives in similar ecosystems.

Nurturing the Tree

At the meeting in New York, tree builders will lay plans to coordinate scattered efforts and graft disparate branches onto a unified tree. "We emphatically cannot go on in an idiosyncratic way," says AMNH Provost Michael Novacek. The scientists also need a truly representative sample of life to build a complete tree.

To that end, the AMNH is collecting hundreds of thousands of animal tissue samples, frozen in 10 cryogenic vats. DNA from the samples, representing every animal lineage, will be sequenced and the information fed into Circe's data-hungry maw. At the meeting, Harvard University biologist Edward Wilson also plans to push for a serious effort to catalog Earth's full diversity of life. The tree builders are likely to endorse his call. Novacek notes that as much as 90 percent of living species remain to be discovered; filling in those gaps, he says, "would provide more clues to the tree of life."

The benefits could flow back to the natural world, by helping researchers identify unique groups, with few neighboring branches, that should become the focus of special conservation efforts. Building a universal tree is the best way to understand the diversity of life. If scientists work fast enough, says Wilson, it might also be the best way to preserve it.

Mother Superior

By Garry Hamilton
New Scientist, September 3, 2005

Have you ever investigated your family tree? Whether it is to learn about our great-grandparents, discover what life was like in the past, or just satisfy our curiosity, there is a growing craze for finding out as much as possible about our ancestors. Genealogy has become one of the top reasons for using the internet (after less wholesome pursuits, of course).

Some people investigate the previous two or three generations of their family; others trace their ancestors over many centuries. But when it comes to extreme genealogy, none can compete with a group of scientists trying to find out about the ancestor of all life.

Every living thing on Earth—from humans to bacteria, from bluebells to blue whales—is thought to be descended from one single entity, a sort of primitive cell floating around in the primordial soup three or four billion years ago. So what did it look like? How did it live, and where? Named the "last universal common ancestor," or LUCA for short, it has left no known fossil remains, nor any other physical clues to its identity. For a long time, questions about LUCA were thought beyond the reach of science.

But LUCA could enjoy a resurrection at last. Researchers are comparing the genes of all kinds of life to draw a portrait of this mother of us all. Their findings are the subject of huge controversy and are challenging some of the most basic assumptions about primordial life. There is evidence, for example, that early evolution was driven by forces very different to those we usually associate with natural selection. Another surprise is that DNA, life's code book, may have evolved on two separate occasions. "This is very exciting," says Anthony Poole of Stockholm University in Sweden. "It changes our picture of LUCA extensively."

It was in the mid-1800s that Charles Darwin first focused attention on our distant ancestry by setting out his theory of evolution by natural selection. He proposed that similar species had common ancestors and so shared a family tree. But Darwin could not decide whether all living creatures belonged to one such tree or several.

It was only in the 1950s and 60s that efforts to probe the most basic operations of cells began unveiling the similarities that link all life forms. Almost every organism, for example, uses long strands of deoxyribonucleic acid, better known as DNA, to encode the countless proteins required to build and sustain life. They also use short lengths of a similar molecule called ribonucleic acid (RNA) for retrieving the information stored in DNA one gene at a time, to allow the proteins to be manufactured. And without exception all life forms use large and complex molecular machines known as ribosomes to use those RNA snippets as templates for assembling proteins out of amino-acid building blocks.

> *Perhaps the most telling evidence for a single common ancestor is the shared language of our genes.*

Perhaps the most telling evidence for a single common ancestor is the shared language of our genes. Although there seem to be no biochemical reasons why certain "letters" of DNA or RNA should encode certain amino acids, the same codes are used across the tree of life, with only a few exceptions (*New Scientist*, 30 August 2003, p 34).

Although LUCA was one of our earliest ancestors, it was not the very first living entity. LUCA's DNA, RNA and ribosomes, almost certainly enclosed by a membrane-bound cell, would have been far too complex to have arisen spontaneously from the primordial soup. The first living entity would have been merely a self-replicating molecule, thought to have arisen around 4.3 billion years ago. It must have slowly evolved into a variety of primitive cells. But only one—LUCA—had descendants that were ultimately successful.

So what did LUCA look like? Our earliest insights came from the work of Carl Woese, a molecular biologist at the University of Illinois in Urbana-Champaign. In the late 1960s he developed a technique for gauging relatedness between species by comparing the sequence of a small segment of RNA found within ribosomes. Assuming genetic mutations accrue over time/the more disparate two species' sequences are, the further back in time the species must have diverged.

Woese's work, which spanned more than a decade, redefined how biologists classify life, in ways that would have a major impact on the search for LUCA. Previously life forms had been divided at the most basic level into two groups: eukaryotes and prokaryotes. Eukaryotes were all animals, plants, fungi and single-celled microbes such as yeast. They consisted of relatively large cells containing many complex internal structures, such as mitochondria for producing energy and a nucleus for housing their DNA, which was wrapped in protein. Prokaryotes, mainly bacteria, comprised smaller, simpler cells, lacking these internal elements but possessing a rigid cell wall made from distinctive sugary proteins called peptidoglycans, not found in eukaryotes.

Woese discovered that within prokaryotes there was actually a third type of creature: a bizarre class of microbes that he named the archaea. Although similar to bacteria in many ways, archaea lack the defining peptidoglycans and possess several eukaryote traits such as having DNA wrapped in protein. From then on scientists adopted a new classification system in which life is divided into three domains: archaea, bacteria—all the prokaryotes that were not archaea—and eukaryotes.

To everyone's surprise, the number of genes shared throughout the tree of life turned out to be remarkably small.

Although a major advance, Woese's early efforts left a key question unanswered: in which order had the three domains evolved? In other words, was LUCA a bacterium, an archaean or a eukaryote? In the late 1980s further comparisons of ribosome RNA suggested bacteria were the oldest domain. Although subsequent analyses of other genes yielded conflicting results, this has remained the prevailing view.

But not everyone subscribes to it. One of the leading naysayers is Patrick Forterre at Paris-Sud University in Orsay, France. He thinks there is a major flaw in the method of such genetic analyses: they fail to take account of the different rates at which mutations can accumulate among different groups. So faster-evolving lineages such as bacteria appear older than they really are.

Bacteria are often assumed to be more primitive than eukaryote cells because they are simpler. But Forterre points out that while eukaryotes are more complex, they are also riddled with what he sees as primitive machinery. For example, eukaryote chromosomes consist of linear strands of DNA that require elaborate molecules called telomeres to protect their ends from damage during replication. Bacterial chromosomes form a loop so they have no need for telomeres.

Eukaryote genes also contain introns—non-coding and often apparently useless DNA whose corresponding sequences must be removed from the intermediary RNA molecules during protein manufacture by complex editing machines known as spliceosomes. Bacteria lack introns so they do not need spliceosomes. In comparison with eukaryotes, bacteria are sleek and efficient at making proteins. They can begin the first step on the road to protein synthesis within seconds; the same events in eukaryotes take half an hour. As such, Forterre argues that bacteria probably evolved more recently, and that LUCA was in fact a eukaryote—one of us.

Elsewhere, a different approach to uncovering LUCA's identity came from the first genome-sequencing projects, completed in the 1990s. These allowed researchers to list the genes that were common to all life forms and so likely to have been passed down from LUCA. But to everyone's surprise, the number of genes shared throughout the tree of life turned out to be remarkably small. The most recent comparison, for example, looked at 100 species and found only 60 genes in common [Nature Reviews Microbiology, vol

1, p 127)—far too few to maintain a cell-based life form such as LUCA, no matter how primitive. It appears that much of the evolutionary record has been erased from species' genomes due to gene loss as organisms adapt to new conditions and ditch redundant genetic material.

Another problem is what is sometimes called horizontal gene transfer. In contrast to the vertical transfer of genes from parent to offspring, single-celled creatures such as bacteria can swap genes between individuals of one generation. Horizontal transfer seems to have played a major role in early evolution. As a result, living species are mosaics of genes with different evolutionary histories.

Hot or Not?

So can we gain any clues about LUCA from where it would have lived? Certain family trees drawn up from gene comparisons suggest the earliest life forms were hyperthermophiles—organisms that live at temperatures over 80 °C. This suggested that LUCA was such a creature too, perhaps living near deep-sea hydrothermal vents, where abundant minerals would have offered an energy source on a planet then lacking oxygen.

This theory's weak point is that life in extreme heat requires special enzymes to protect RNA and DNA from damage. It seems more probable that simpler life forms first arose at moderate temperatures before evolving the enzymes that allowed them to gradually nudge closer to hot zones. And recent research has further undermined the theory. Work done in 2000 showed that reverse gyrase, an enzyme that appears to boost DNA's resistance to heat damage and is found only in hyperthermophiles, did not evolve until after the three domains had split. Meanwhile, other protective genes found in bacteria appear to have been horizontally acquired from archaea.

A more direct challenge to the theory that LUCA was a heat lover comes from recent work by Celine Brochier and Herve Philippe, evolutionary biologists then at the Pierre and Marie Curie University in Paris, France. They argue that previous work on ribosome RNA was flawed because it included rapidly evolving genetic material, which is more likely to have lost useful historical information. Instead they focused on the more slowly evolving parts of ribosome RNA. In 2002 they published a tree that suggests the oldest living organisms are an unusual group of bacteria known as Planctomycetales, which survive only at moderate temperatures (Nature, vol 417, p 244). These organisms lack peptidoglycan in their cell walls and their chromosomes are enclosed in a membrane, the closest thing in bacteria to a cell nucleus.

But not everyone agrees. Molecular biologist Massimo Di Giulio at the International Institute of Genetics and Biophysics in Naples, Italy, believes Brochier and Philippe failed to use enough material from the ribosome RNA to make their analysis meaningful. Di Giulio repeated the French team's work using more genetic material and got different results. In the tree he drew, Planctomycetales were still near the base, but two groups of extreme heat lovers—Aquificales and Thermotogales—proved even more ancient. The debate is currently at an impasse, stalled by the uncertainty over whose methods are more accurate.

Even the very nature of LUCA's genes has come into question. It has long been thought that the first self-replicating organisms

> *"What it really looks like is that DNA has evolved twice."*—Anthony Poole, **Stockholm University**

could not have used today's system of DNA and proteins because it is too complex and interdependent to have arisen spontaneously. DNA encodes the proteins that catalyse the chemical reactions that replicate DNA—one could not exist without the other. So the first genes were probably made of RNA, which, due to its different chemical properties, can catalyse some reactions without proteins. This "RNA world" would eventually have been superseded by the superior DNA/protein system, with RNA relegated to its present accessory role. LUCA, it was first thought, could only have existed after the DNA/protein stage had been reached because all life forms seemed to make and use DNA in the same way. For example, the enzyme ribonucleotide reductase, which organisms use to create the building blocks for DNA, contains a molecular core that is identical in all three domains. "It's like looking at triplets," says Poole.

But recent genome comparisons have uncovered a list of differences in the molecular machinery associated with DNA in the three domains. Some of the enzymes that bacteria use for replicating DNA, for example, are unrelated to the ones used by archaea and eukaryotes. Poole and others now believe the most likely explanation is that LUCA existed before the switch from RNA genes to DNA ones occurred. "What it really looks like," says Poole, "is that DNA has evolved twice."

If that were not heresy enough, Carl Woese, whose work identified the domain of archaea, has recently cast doubt on whether LUCA even existed. He argues that the last common ancestor was not an individual organism, but a varied community of horizontally gene-swapping primitive cells.

The earliest membrane-bound cells would have been extremely simple, Woese argues, comprising a few basic components that could function independently if their genes were acquired individually by other cells. Horizontal gene transfer would have been the main power behind evolution at this point, not vertical inheritance. "There would have been a time when gene transfer was the dominant evolutionary force," says Woese.

As cells became more complex, individual components acquired at random could not be so easily incorporated. At this point, which Woese calls the Darwinian threshold, genomes began to depend on inheritance, and lineages with distinct identities began to emerge from the communal soup. Woese thinks this theory is the best explanation of the fact that the tree of life looks different depending on which genes you choose to analyse.

But other scientists have not given up on LUCA and are trying to understand the inconsistencies by developing better analytical tools. At the National Center for Biotechnology Information in Bethesda, Maryland, evolutionary biologist Eugene Koonin has recently renewed attempts to compile a list of LUCA's genes. His team has developed a computer model for determining the relative roles played by gene loss and horizontal gene transfer, and so far they have identified about 600 candidate genes.

Koonin and others hope to discover the minimum genes required to run a primitive cell so this minimal genome can be assembled in the lab. "It is easy to imagine a 'Jurassic Park' of cellular evolution, with experimental study of various reconstructed ancestral forms," wrote Koonin in a recent paper.

Clearly the search for LUCA is only just hotting up.

Evo Devo

By Gareth Cook
The Boston Globe, March 13, 2006

To understand one of the latest theories in evolution, consider the "Iron Chef" television show.

Dueling chefs are given a featured ingredient and then race to create dishes. They both start with, say, lobster meat, but one might produce a seaweed salad while the other would make corn and lobster dumplings.

Substitute genes for ingredients, and it explains how humans can be so similar to chimpanzees—sharing more than 98 percent of our genetic code—and yet so different. In becoming human, people didn't evolve a lot of new genes, scientists believe; they made different use of the ones they had.

In December, researchers at Duke University announced some of the first concrete evidence for this idea. They focused on a gene that makes a protein involved in memory and perception. Although the protein is exactly the same in human and chimpanzee brains, the team found that humans have evolved minute genetic changes that cause brain cells to make, or "express," more of the crucial protein, perhaps helping the human brain to work better. A little more of these proteins here, a little less of those proteins there, and voila a chimp becomes a human.

The chimpanzee research is part of a profound conceptual shift. Biologists have long suspected that "gene expression"—the way cells make more of some proteins and less of others—could be important in answering many biological questions. But now some biologists believe that this process could play a vital role in explaining the way one species evolves into another with sometimes shocking speed.

"What we used to think of as big, complex changes are in fact remarkably easy to achieve" through changes in gene expression, said Gregory A. Wray, a professor of biology at Duke University who led the chimpanzee research. "This is changing the way that we think about evolution."

The new research on gene expression could provide an answer to a puzzle that has confounded biologists since Darwin and that has recently been seized on by proponents of intelligent design: the idea that life is too complex to have happened without the help of a higher being. With the "survival of the fittest," it is easy to see that a lion that runs a little faster will be a better hunter and thus be more likely to survive and pass on this attribute to its offspring. Over time, these improvements accumulate, and lions evolve.

But where do these changes come from in the first place? In other words, how could it be that a single, random genetic change would be able to improve on something so complex as, say, the legs of a lion, with all of their interconnected joints, tendons, nerves, and muscles.

"We need to understand how you get the various kinds of novelty—the first hand, the first eye, the first brain," said Marc Kirschner at a recent talk at Harvard Medical School, where he is a professor. "It is the variety of life that needs explaining." Kirschner is co-author of a new book, "The Plausibility of Life," about the biological sources of evolutionary change.

The research on gene expression, and particularly an active field called "evolutionary developmental biology," or "evo devo," is now addressing this question, according to Sean B. Carroll, a scientist at the University of Wisconsin-Madison and the Howard Hughes Medical Institute.

In every cell, there are genes that create the proteins that are the building blocks of life.

In every cell, there are genes that create the proteins that are the building blocks of life. But these proteins can also work as signals, turning on or off other genes. The proteins from these genes may affect still more genes. So a protein from a single gene can set off a cascade of other changes. A study published in *Nature* last week by scientists at Yale University found that as humans evolved from their ape ancestors, the regulatory genes were more likely to have changed than genes that don't switch other genes.

Changes in gene expression are particularly important during embryonic development. One small, accidental genetic change, Carroll and others say, can cause changes in the expression of many genes, which change how the body of an animal develops before it is born. For example, changing a single gene in the fruit fly will cause it to grow a leg on its head instead of an antenna. In a sense, the mutation has changed the biological signal that means "grow an antenna here" to "grow a leg here." Sometimes, such a genetic change and all the physical changes it causes will leave the animal better adapted to its surroundings, and evolution takes off.

Biologists widely agree that gene expression is important, but its role in evolution is still very much an open question because researchers only recently began finding clear examples.

One of their more remarkable discoveries is research published on what have come to be called "Darwin's finches." When Charles Darwin's ship, the *Beagle*, came upon the Galapagos Islands off the coast of Ecuador in 1835, the young naturalist was particularly amazed by the finches. Across the islands, the brown-feathered birds looked similar, but their beaks were different.

In some of the species, the finches had beaks that were broad and stout, ideal for cracking through tough seeds, while in others the beaks were more pointed, ideal for reaching the pollen in flowers or piercing fruits. The finches, Darwin surmised, had begun as one species but then separated into the species he saw, each with a beak adapted to take advantage of particular foods in its environment. The finches helped inspire Darwin's theory of evolution.

In 2004, a team led by Harvard Medical School professor Cliff Tabin showed that many of the complex changes in the beak—a stouter structure that must meet reshaped bones of the skull— could be explained by a single genetic switch. When a particular gene, called Bmp4, turned on earlier in the development of the beak, the finches ended up with the stouter beaks, according to a paper in the journal *Science*. His team, which included Arhat Abzhanov of Harvard Medical School, verified the finding by artificially activating the gene earlier in a developing chicken. The chicken's beak looked more like one of Darwin's seed-cracking finches.

Tabin's team did not identify what caused the gene to come on earlier in some finches, but the gene is known to signal other genes to become more or less active. Such genes, known as regulatory genes, act like the choreographers of a developing animal. In a sense, the gene can be thought of like a dial: Turn it up, and the entire beak structure morphs one way; turn it down, and the beak morphs another way.

This, then, explains how small random genetic changes could create a coordinated set of changes that might make for a better adapted animal. It is just a twist of a dial, triggered by an accidental genetic change.

Other scientists have discovered similar systems at work in the evolution of other forms of life. Carroll, author of a recent book on evo devo, "Endless Forms Most Beautiful," has documented shifts in regulatory genes that change the patterns of spots on fruit flies. John Doebley, another scientist at the University of Wisconsin-Madison, has identified small changes that helped the teosinte, a plant that looks like a large grass, develop into maize, the plant with dramatic ears that was a key source of food for Native Americans.

Another example is the dramatic increase in the size of human brains compared with the brains of their ape cousins, according to Dr. Christopher A. Walsh, chief of genetics at Children's Hospital Boston. He helped identify a gene that, when mutated, causes children to be born with brains less than half the normal size—comparable, in fact, to the size of a chimpanzee brain. What is remarkable about the disease, called microcephaly, is that it is not deadly. It is debilitating, but patients can learn to walk on their own and sometimes even speak a few words.

It seems likely, Walsh suggested, that changes in this one gene, long ago, may have helped humans develop larger brains. The gene does not appear to be involved in regulating other genes, but it shows how a relatively small change can have a dramatic effect.

Although Walsh and other scientists are using the latest tools of genetics, they are following the trail of a question that has been around since well before Darwin's time: how to explain the sheer richness of life, from ivory-tusked elephants to bumble bees, from humans to humming birds. The slow accumulation of new genes over many millions of years is a crucial part of the answer. But so are the tiny changes that cause something dramatic and new to spring to life.

Humans, Chimps May Have Bred After Split

By Gareth Cook
The Boston Globe, May 18, 2006

Boston scientists released a provocative report yesterday that challenges the timeline of human evolution and suggests that human ancestors bred with chimpanzee ancestors long after they had initially separated into two species.

The researchers, working at the Cambridge-based Broad Institute of Harvard and MIT, used a wealth of newly available genetic data to estimate the time when the first human ancestors split from the chimpanzees. The team arrived at an answer that is at least 1 million years later than paleontologists had believed, based on fossils of early, humanlike creatures.

The lead scientist said that this jarring conflict with the fossil record, combined with a number of other strange genetic patterns the team uncovered, led him to a startling explanation: that human ancestors evolved apart from the chimpanzees for hundreds of thousands of years, and then started breeding with them again before a final break.

"Something very unusual happened," said David Reich, one of the report's authors and a geneticist at the Broad and Harvard Medical School.

The suggestion of interbreeding was met with skepticism by paleontologists, who said they had trouble imagining a successful breeding between early human ancestors, which walked upright, and the chimpanzee ancestors, which walked on all fours. But other scientists said the work is impressive and will probably force a reappraisal of the story of human origins. And one leading paleontologist said he welcomed the research as a sign that new genetic information will yield more clues to our deep history than once thought.

"I find this terrifically exciting and important work," said David Pilbeam, a Harvard paleontologist who was not part of the Broad team.

Pilbeam helped discover an early human ancestor known as Toumai, which walked on two legs and is thought to have lived in present-day Chad 6.5 million to 7.4 million years ago. The new report, published in today's issue of the journal *Nature*, estimates that final break between the human and chimpanzee species did not come until 6.3 million years ago at the earliest, and probably less than 5.4 million years ago.

This contradiction could be resolved, Reich said, if early creatures like Toumai then interbred with chimpanzee ancestors, leaving a population of hybrids that developed into today's humans. (In this scenario, the line of Toumai creatures then went extinct.) But it is also possible, he said, that the dating of the early human fossils is wrong, or that the dating of other, older fossils used in his calculations is wrong, which would partially undercut the interbreeding theory. Scientists said that the report will probably bring intense scrutiny, as researchers look for potential flaws in the work or other explanations for its findings.

It is not known why human ancestors would have begun mating with chimpanzee ancestors again, or why they would have stopped.

The work will also probably inspire biologists to devote more attention to hybrids, the term for offspring with parents of different species, and the role that they may play in fueling evolution. Biologists have long known about hybrids—a half-grizzly bear, half-polar bear was recently discovered in Canada—but it has been assumed that these were generally lone animals that had had little impact on the story of evolution. The *Nature* paper joins a wave of work showing that the lines between species are hazy, according to James Mallet, a biologist who studies hybrids at University College London.

As two species evolve, they can develop new abilities. Some hybrids could combine the best of both species, Mallet said, though the biological barriers to the creation of hybrids increase the longer the species are apart. It is thought that human ancestors were adapting to life on the savannah instead of the forest, where chimpanzees still live today. It is not known why human ancestors would have begun mating with chimpanzee ancestors again, or why they would have stopped.

To understand how long ago humans split from chimpanzees, Reich and his colleagues did a close study of DNA from the two. This technique rests on the idea that once the populations separate, the DNA will slowly drift apart as natural mutations accumulate. If they can count the number of changes, and determine how quickly the changes happened, then they can calculate how long the two populations have been separate, according to Nick Patterson, a scientist who was part of the Broad team.

Previous studies have used this idea and found that the two species split between about 5 million and 8 million years ago.

The Broad team sought to get a more precise answer by looking at how different the DNA of chimps and humans is at many locations, instead of calculating an average difference. The DNA of humans and chimpanzees is quite similar, meaning that scientists can readily identify many segments of DNA that are so similar they must have been handed down by a common ancestor, deep in the past. Scientists can then use a computer to put the segments of human and chimp DNA into alignment, placing side by side the segments that are very similar.

For each pair of segments, they then calculated how long it would have taken to accumulate all the differences. The team used sophisticated statistical techniques to calculate these "divergence times."

This analysis brought surprises that the team could explain only by suggesting human ancestors and chimpanzee ancestors interbred. First, they found that the divergence times varied widely. Some parts of the DNA seemed to indicate the human and chimpanzee species had been apart much longer than others, by millions of years. If humans split from chimps and then interbred before splitting again, the more divergent DNA sequences could date to before the first split, while the less divergent sequences could date to just before the second split.

The other surprise was that sequences from the X chromosome, one of two chromosomes that determine gender, gave consistently more recent divergence times, instead of the range seen on other chromosomes. This, too, would be explained by the idea of interbreeding, according to the report. The X chromosome is thought to be the focus of fertility problems in hybrids, and population models suggest that all of the X chromosomes in a hybrid population would quickly come to match those of one of the parent species. This would explain why the human and chimpanzee X chromosomes are so similar.

Although the idea is controversial, there will soon be a wealth of more information to test it. Part of the Broad team's analysis relied on using DNA sequences from the gorilla and other primates as a kind of baseline to interpret their results. Only a relatively small amount of DNA has been sequenced from gorillas, limiting the amount of data the team could use. By the end of 2007, there should be a full sequence of the gorilla, allowing the scientists to do a much fuller analysis, Reich said.

The team also plans on looking at genetic data for other groups of closely related species to try to determine whether those species split apart fairly abruptly, or whether there is evidence that hybridization is a common part of evolution, bringing together the best of two species.

IV. The Fossil Record

Editors' Introduction

Before the late 18th century, it was generally believed that all of the earth's creatures were immutable, perfect in their original creation. Consequently, it was inconceivable that any species would ever become extinct. "Fossils had no fundamental significance: Such things were simply sports of nature or remnants of some still-living species," Edward J. Larson wrote in *Evolution* (2004). This notion fell with the invention of the field of paleontology. After the French naturalist Georges Cuvier accepted a position with the Museum of Natural History in Paris, in 1795, he began comparing reconstructed fossilized remains with those of modern animals and determined that the fossils belonged to ancient species that no longer roamed the earth.

Today much of our understanding of our planet's biological history is drawn from the fossil record—the remains or traces of plants or animals that have been preserved in the earth's crust. While most organic remains deteriorate shortly after an organism's death, on rare occasions, when environmental conditions are precisely right, the hard parts of buried remains—such as teeth, claws, shells, and bones—become petrified and turn to stone as the minerals from the soil replace the organic matter. In even rarer cases, some of the soft tissue is also preserved.

Given the unique circumstances required for fossilization, it is estimated that less than one percent of all the species that have ever existed have been fossilized, according Donald R. Prothero in "The Fossils Say Yes." Creationists often note that the fossil record is woefully incomplete and argue that it is therefore of questionable value. While Prothero acknowledges that it is far from perfect, he points out that the fossil record not only is bolstered by DNA evidence but also contains numerous transitional fossils—or "missing links," as they are more commonly known—that support evolutionary theory.

One such transitional form was recently discovered in the barren fjords of arctic Canada. In "Fossil Discovery Fills Gap in Evolutionary Path from Fish to Land Animals," Richard Montastersky reports that while this newfound creature possessed fins and scales like a fish, it also had a neck—an anatomical feature not found on any fossil or living fish—an elbow joint, and even a primitive wrist-like structure. These adaptations may have allowed the creature to drag itself out of the water and across mud flats, much in the manner of the modern mudskipper.

Until recently scientists had yet to discover any transitional forms for the more than 80 species of mammals that are classified as whales, leading to a great deal of speculation about their origins. Recent fossil discoveries, however, indicate that they are derived from a furry, four-legged creature with hooves at the end of its four-toed feet. In "Evolution of Whales," Douglas H. Chadwick discusses how whales evolved from such a seemingly disparate form.

Paleontologsts believe that modern birds descended from theropods, a group of bipedal, meat-eating dinosaurs that included such species as the tyrannosaur and velociraptor. As William Mullen reports in "Little Meat-eater Is No Bird, but Close," the recent discovery of a fossil from a suborder of theropods that is closely related to bird ancestors could force scientists to redraw evolutionary charts. This turkey-sized, carnivorous bird is the oldest of it kind to be found and the first discovered in South America.

In the final article of this chapter, "The Astonishing Micropygmies," the evolutionary biologist and Pulitzer Prize–winning author Jared Diamond discusses the startling discovery of the remains of tiny humans on the Indonesian island of Flores. These micropygmies—or hobbits, as they have been nicknamed—stood only three feet high and are believed to have descended from *Homo erectus*. Some of the remains from the Flores site indicate that this species lived as recently as 18,000 years ago, which surprised scientists, who had believed that all human forms besides *Homo sapiens* had died out thousands of years earlier.

The Fossils Say Yes

By Donald R. Prothero
Natural History, November 2005

> "It has been asserted over and over again, by writers who believe in the immutability of species, that geology yields no linking forms. This assertion . . . is certainly erroneous. . . . What geological research has not revealed, is the former existence of infinitely numerous gradations . . . connecting together nearly all existing and extinct species."

> —*Charles Darwin,* The Origin of Species

When Darwin first proposed the idea of evolution by natural selection in 1859, the fossil record offered little support for his ideas. Darwin even devoted two entire chapters of the Origin of Species to the imperfection of the geologic record, because he was well aware it was one of the weakest links in his arguments. Then, just two years after his book was published, the first specimen of Archaeopteryx was discovered, hailed by many as the "missing link" between birds and reptiles. By the late nineteenth century, fossils helped demonstrate how the modern thoroughbred horse evolved from a dog-size, three-toed creature with low-crowned teeth. (The understanding of those fossils has since been much refined.)

Fossil evidence supporting evolution has continued to mount, particularly in the past few decades. DNA analysis, moreover, has helped make sense of how the evidence fits together in the family tree of life on Earth. Unfortunately, many people still think, quite erroneously, that the fossil-record shows no "transitional forms." In large part, that misconception is the product of the campaign of misinformation—or disinformation—spread by the creationist movement.

The fossil record is far from perfect, of course. By most estimates, less than 1 percent of all the species that have ever lived are preserved as fossils. The reason for the scarcity is simply that the physical conditions needed to turn a dead organism into a fossil lasting millions of years are unusual.

Nevertheless, there are numerous excellent specimens that reflect transitional stages between major groups of organisms. Many more fossils exhibit how "infinitely numerous gradations" connect the species. The one caveat is that when a sequence of fossils appears to follow a direct line of descent, the chances are slim that they actually bear such precise interrelations. Paleontologists recognize that when one fossil looks ancestral to another, the first fossil is more safely described as being closely related to the actual ancestor.

The classic story of the evolution of the horse is a good example. The various known fossils were once arranged—simplistically, it turns out—into a single lineage leading from "Eohippus" to Equus. When more fossils became available, paleontologists revised that simple lineage. The fossils now give a branching and very bushy picture of equine evolution, with numerous now-extinct lineages living side by side. One quarry in Nebraska has yielded a dozen distinct species of fossil horses, in rock about 12 million years old. The earliest horses, such as Protorohippus (from early in the Eocene epoch, about 53 million years ago), are virtually indistinguishable from Homogalax, the earliest member of the lineage, which also gave rise to tapirs and rhinoceroses. Very early in my career, when I was taking an undergraduate paleontology class, I discovered just how tough it is to sort out those two ancient genera.

Perhaps the most remarkable recent discoveries are the numerous fossils that connect whales with their four-legged terrestrial ancestors.

Perhaps the most remarkable recent discoveries are the numerous fossils that connect whales with their four-legged terrestrial ancestors. If you look at dolphins, orcas, and blue whales, all fully aquatic animals, you would have a hard time imagining them walking on land. Yet even living whales retain vestiges of their hips and thighbones, deeply buried in the muscles along their spines. Paleontologists have known for a long time, on the basis of detailed features of the skull and teeth, that whales are closely related to hoofed mammals. But creationists long touted the absence of transitional fossils for whales as evidence against evolution.

The balance has now changed. In 1983 specimens of Pakicetus were discovered Pakistan in early Eocene beds about 52 million years old. Although the body of Pakicetus was primarily terrestrial, it had the skull and teeth of the ancient archaeocetes, the earliest family of whales—which swam the world's oceans in the Middle Eocene epoch, about 50 million years ago.

Then, in 1994, Ambulocetus natans (literally, the "walking whale that swims") was discovered, also in Pakistan. The animal was the size of a large sea lion, with broad webbed feet on both fore and hind limbs, so it could both walk and swim. Yet it still had tiny hooves on its toes and the primitive skull and teeth of the archaeocete. Ambulocetus apparently swam much like an otter, with an up-and-down motion of the spine, the precursor to the motion of the flukes of a whale's tail. In 1995 yet a third transitional, creature was discovered. Dalanistes, with shorter legs than Ambulocetus, webbed feet; a longer tail, and a much larger and more whalelike skull.

Today more than a dozen transitional whale fossils have been unearthed—an excellent series for such rarely fossilized animals. DNA from the living species suggests that whales are descended from even toed hoofed mammals known as artiodactyls and, in particular, are most closely related to the hippopotamus. That hypothesis was dramatically confirmed by the discoveries in 2001 of the "double-pulley" anklebone, which is characteristic of artiodactyls, in two kinds of primitive whales.

Whales are not the only aquatic mammals with terrestrial ancestors. Modern sirenians (manatees and dugongs) are large, docile, aquatic herbivores that have flippers for forelimbs and no hind limbs. In 2001 Daryl Domning, a marine mammal paleontologist at Howard University in Washington, D.C., described a remarkably complete skeleton of Pezosiren portelli from Jamaican deposits about 50 million years old. That animal had the typical skull and teeth of a sirenian, and even the thick sirenian ribs made of dense bone, which serve as ballast. Yet it had four legs as well, all with feet, not flippers. Strong transitional fossils also link seals and sea lions to bearlike ancestors.

The origin of mammals is well documented. Mammals and their extinct relatives belong to a larger group known as the Synapsida. The earliest members of the group were once known as "mammal-like reptiles," even though they were not true reptiles but had already evolved to become a separate branch of animals. Among them was Dimetrodon, the largest predator on Earth about 280 million years ago. (Its sail-shaped back is familiar from toy-dinosaur kits for children, even though it was not a true dinosaur.) Although it was a primitive form, Dimetrodon had large, stabbing canine teeth and some of the specialized skull features of mammals.

For the next 80 million years, synapsids evolved into various wolflike and bearlike predators, as well as into an array of peculiar piglike herbivores. Along the way, they acquired progressively more mammalian features: additional jaw muscles that enabled complex chewing motions; a secondary palate covering the old reptilian palate and nasal region, which enabled them to breathe and eat at the same time; multicusped molars for chewing rather than gulping their food; enlarged brains; relatively upright (rather than sprawling) posture; and a muscular diaphragm in the rib cage for efficient breathing. There are even signs that they had hair, a quintessentially mammalian feature. The story of the synapsids culminates in the appearance of the earliest true mammals— shrew-size creatures—in fossil beds about 200 million years old in China, South Africa, and Texas.

Among the most remarkable transformations that took place as the mammals emerged are the ones that can be observed in fossils of the lower jaws. In reptiles and primitive synapsids, the right and left lower jaws are each made up of a number of bones, one of which is the dentary, or tooth-bearing, bone. As synapsids evolved, the dentary bone grew progressively larger until it took over the role of hinging the jaw to the skull. One of the other reptilian jawbones shrank until it vanished, whereas the other two shifted to the middle ear. There they became the anvil and the hammer, minute bones that transmit sound from the eardrum to the stirrup bone and, ultimately, to the inner ear. The shift in function seems bizarre until you realize that in reptiles, sound vibrations from the lower jaw travel through the skull bones to the inner ear, and that, along with the vibrations that travel from the eardrum, those vibrations are important sources of sensation.

> *Many fossil species show the transition from dinosaurs to birds.*

Excellent "missing links" now exist for other major groups as well. Many fossil species show the transition from dinosaurs to birds. Archaeopteryx, for instance, discovered in Europe in Late Jurassic fossil beds about 150 million years old, had teeth. Slightly younger fossils, from the Chinese Lower Cretaceous, about 140 million years ago, had more birdlike features. Sinornis, for instance, had wings it could fold against its body, grasping feet with an opposable toe, and tailbones fused into a single element. Confuciusornis sported the first toothless beak. Lower Cretaceous rocks in Spain, about 130 million years old, have yielded Iberomesornis, which had a large, keeled breastbone to which powerful flight muscles were anchored. Still, the creature had the primitive long backbone of a dinosaur.

Such bird fossils are now joined in the web of ancient life-forms by numerous, recently discovered fossils of nonflying, nonavian dinosaurs, closely related to Velociraptor of Jurassic Park fame. Those fossils, such as Microraptor and Caudipteryx, had well-developed feathers, suggesting that feathers originally served other functions, such as insulation, long before they became useful for flight [see "Bird's-eye View," by Matthew T. Carrano and Patrick M. O'Connor, May 2005].

Another transition that is now well documented is the conquest of the land by the amphibians. For decades the only good intermediate fossil between fishes and amphibians was Ichthyostega, from the Late Devonian epoch (about 360 million years ago) of Greenland and Spitzbergen. Although Ichthyostega resembled many amphibians in having well-developed legs, a complete shoulder girdle, and hips fused to the backbone, it still had fishlike gill slits, a sensory system on its face for detecting underwater currents, and a long, fishlike tail fin.

More recent discoveries, such as Acanthostega from the same beds, show that the picture is much more complicated and interesting. Acanthostega had ear bones that were still adapted for underwater hearing, a longer tail fin than Ichthyostega, and better-developed gills, making it more primitive and aquatic than Ichthyostega. Acanthostega also had as many as eight toes on each of its four feet—rather than five, which became the standard in most early four-footed creatures.

> *The human fossil record has become quite dense and complete, and the newfound samples have led to some surprises.*

Apparently, its limbs were primarily adapted for swimming and walking along the bottom of a lake, rather than for crawling on land. Contrary to the popular story that four legs evolved because they enabled animals to crawl out onto the land (to escape drying ponds, chase new food sources, and so forth); it now appears that legs evolved for walking underwater (as most salamanders still do today). They became secondarily useful on land, because they were already in place.

What about the transitional forms that led to our favorite species, Homo sapiens? Not long ago, the fossil record of the human family was severely limited, and readily thrown into confusion by a single fraudulent "fossil" such as the 1912 hoax known as Piltdown Man. But in the past three decades new findings have exploded. In Chad, fossils of Sahelanthropus were discovered in beds between 6 million and 7 million years old. In Ethiopia, the new genus Ardipithecus and two new species of Australopithecus (A. anamensis and A. bahrelghazali) were unearthed in beds between 2 million and 5 million years old. Several species of our own genus, Homo, which goes back at least 2 million years, have now been identified.

In short, the human fossil record has become quite dense and complete, and the newfound samples have led to some surprises. For example, contrary to the expectations of earlier anthropologists, the fossils show that bipedalism arose before enlarged brains, which came quite late in human evolution.

The origin of vertebrates as a whole once also presented a frustrating gap in the fossil record. Biologists could examine the many living animals (such as lancelets and sea squirts) that represented stages in the transition from the invertebrates to the earliest jawless fishes. Until recently, however, few good fossils had been identified from beds older than about 480 million years, near the beginning of the Ordovician period. What's more, they were only scattered bony scales and plates.

But recent discoveries in China from the Middle Cambrian epoch, between 510 million and 500 million years ago, have included not only the earliest relatives of the lancelets, but also some soft-bodied specimens that appear to be the earliest vertebrates. Thus, back-boned animals can now be traced all the way back to the Cambrian, when most of the modern branches of animals originated.

As the 150th anniversary of Darwin's Origin approaches, the fossil evidence now available would make Darwin proud, rather than apologetic. Evolutionary biologists can also look forward to many more discoveries. Some will come as a surprise, like the early small-brained bipedal hominids. Some will force paleontologists to revise their ideas about evolutionary events. But the fossil record is no longer the embarrassment that it was in Darwin's day.

Fossil Discovery Fills Gap in Evolutionary Path from Fish to Land Animals

By Richard Monastersky
The Chronicle of Higher Education, April 14, 2006

While prospecting in the barren fjords of Arctic Canada, a trio of paleontologists struck the evolutionary equivalent of gold. They uncovered three specimens of a 383-million-year-old creature midway between fish and land animals, providing a unique snapshot of the process that allowed our aquatic ancestors to crawl out of rivers and colonize the continents.

"This is incredible," says Neil H. Shubin, a professor and chairman of the department of organismal biology and anatomy at the University of Chicago and a member of the team that excavated the fossils on Ellesmere Island, in the Nunavut territory. "We'd pinch ourselves every day that we were removing these things. We couldn't believe it."

Mr. Shubin made the discovery in 2004 with Edward B. Daeschler, of the Academy of Natural Sciences, in Philadelphia, and Farish A. Jenkins Jr., of Harvard University. They described the new species last week in the journal Nature.

The newfound fossil looks like a mosaic, combining some features of a fish and other characteristics of a tetrapod, the group of animals with four limbs that includes humans. The creature had fins and scales on its back like a fish, but it had a neck, a feature not seen on living or fossil fish. It also had an elbow joint and the makings of a primitive wrist, revealing that it could have propped its body up and lumbered over the mud flats, says Mr. Shubin. They named the creature Tiktaalik roseae after the word for fish in the local language in Nunavut.

Tiktaalik is helping scientists work out the evolution of tetrapods because it falls smack into a fossil gap in the late Devonian period. In rocks just a few million years older, researchers find a predatory fish called Panderichthys that had shoulders adapted to pushing its way through shallow water. Then, 17 million years after Tiktaalik, there were creatures with well-developed limbs, complete with fingers and toes, that lived much of their lives out of the water. But until now, researchers have lacked evidence about what happened in between those two times.

"Here suddenly, we get a good animal that's not quite in the middle of the gap but narrows it quite considerably," says Per Erik Ahlberg, a professor of evolutionary and organismal biology at Uppsala University, in Sweden.

Evolutionary Icon

In a commentary in Nature, Mr. Ahlberg and Jennifer A. Clack, of the University of Cambridge, compare the new fish to Archaeopteryx, one of the most famous fossils and the earliest known bird. Tiktaalik is a "link between fishes and land vertebrates that might in time become as much of an evolutionary icon as the proto-bird Archaeopteryx," they write.

During the Devonian period, this part of Canada had the polar opposite climate. It was tropical or subtropical, with lazy rivers meandering through the region. Tiktaalik's adaptations would have helped it in this environment, says Robert L. Carroll, a professor of biology and curator of vertebrate paleontology at the Redpath Museum, at McGill University.

In other fish, the head is connected strongly to the trunk of the body and cannot move separately. But Tiktaalik had a neck and could move its head separately, an advantage in shallow water where fish could not easily tilt their trunks to get their heads up into the air.

The Canadian fossil also shows evidence of having lost the bony cheek flaps that help draw water through the gills. "It likely relied on gulping air," says Mr. Shubin.

The researchers are going back to Ellesmere Island this summer and plan on looking at slightly younger rocks to see if they can find creatures more advanced than Tiktaalik. The scientists can only reach their site by helicopter, and they have found so many fossils that one of their biggest challenges is deciding which of the heavy fossils to bring home and which to leave out in the frozen Canadian wilderness.

Evolution of Whales

By Douglas H. Chadwick
National Geographic, November 2001

The coast of southern Alaska grows glaciers and brooding rain forests. Hot weather is rare, but since sunup the day had brought nothing else. By afternoon everyone was sweltering. The first person to do more than just talk about leaping off the boat into iceberg-chilled Frederick Sound performed a cannonball. Others jack-knifed and belly flopped in. This contest to raise the biggest splash was spirited but short. No sooner had the last person shivered back aboard than three humpback whales surfaced exactly where the jumpers had been landing. The whales lingered a while, misting the crew with spray from their blowholes, then eased down out of sight.

We were still exclaiming about the visit minutes later when the sea to starboard erupted. A 45-foot whale went skyborne up to its tail. Then a pair leaped in near synchrony. Shwaboom! Ker-bloosh! Others started to breach on all sides. For the next half hour humpbacks were flying and crash-landing, sending out minor tsunamis, floating head down to whap the water with their tail flukes, and lying on their sides to slap the surface with long pectoral fins.

It would be the height of arrogance to think we inspired 40-ton organic submarines to compete with us. But I saw what I saw. Whales have a way of making the incredible real; their very name has become a metaphor for something almost too big to get our minds around. I wondered what the crews on whaling ships thought when they would occasionally haul aboard a fully grown adult with miniature legs sticking out from its flanks. Whether they knew it or not, they were looking at testimony to the origin of these mysterious marine giants.

More than 80 living species of mammals are classified as whales, or, as taxonomists say, cetaceans (from ketos, the Greek name for sea monster). They can be divided into two groups. Mysticetes, or baleen whales, use comblike plates hanging from the roofs of their mouths to strain food from seawater. Blue whales, fin whales, bowheads, and most of the other real titans belong to this division along with smaller types such as minke whales and pygmy right whales. Odontocetes, or toothed whales, include belugas, narwhals, sperm whales, pilot whales, and beaked whales—plus all the dolphins and porpoises. We call the largest dolphins killer whales.

But what did the first whales look like? And what gave rise to them? For a long time scientists could only speculate, for the oldest fossils anyone knew of had already assumed the basic appearance of whales. In the absence of intermediate forms, people proposed almost every type of mammal as ancestors.

At last a series of fossil discoveries has unveiled whales' distant past. Paleontologists can suddenly trace the most colossal animals ever to appear on Earth step-by-step back to their beginnings early in the Eocene epoch, often referred to as the dawn of the age of mammals, which lasted from about 55 million to 34 million years ago.

The largest cetaceans, blue whales, may span a hundred feet and weigh a third of a million pounds, larger than any dinosaur dimensions; their skulls wouldn't fit into most rooms. When I visited Hans Thewissen at Northeastern Ohio Universities College of Medicine, he showed me one of the oldest known whales by placing its skull in my outstretched hand. At first glance I thought he had handed me the head of a coyote.

The skull belonged to a relatively small, furry, four-legged meat-eater, one that walked on hooves and died around 50 million years ago. The fossil, named Pakicetus, was unearthed in the Himalayan foothills from sediments whose other contents tell us that the creature lived with land dwellers that included marsupials and our own very early ancestors, squirrel-size primates.

Its remains are closely linked with river channels, suggesting a life spent partly in the water. What causes scientists to declare the creature a whale? Subtle clues in combination—the arrangement of cusps on the molar teeth, a folding in a bone of the middle ear, and the positioning of the ear bones within the skull—are absent in other land mammals but a signature of later Eocene whales.

A million years after Pakicetus a relative took up life at the edge of the sea. Thewissen discovered the fossil in Pakistan in 1994 and named it Ambulocetus natans, the walking, swimming whale. It had thick, splayed-out legs, four-toed feet, and a little hoof at the end of each toe.

As soon as I saw the limbs laid out with the rest of the skeleton, I knew I wouldn't have wanted to go wading in Ambulocetus territory. Squat, powerful, sharp of tooth, and roughly the size of a large sea lion, this whale-in-progress may have been an ambush hunter, lying submerged like a shaggy crocodile, then leaping forth to snatch passing prey.

The next time I met Thewissen, it was on a desert plain in western India known as the Rann of Kutch. With Sunil Bajpai, an early-whale expert from the University of Roorkee, we set off into a landscape of camels and goats, where jackals panted in the thorn-scrub shade. Some 45 million to 42 million years earlier Kutch was a green, shifting border of a river delta, periodically drowned by the ancient Tethys Sea. The place rippled with sharks, rays, bony fish, crocodiles, and turtles, as well as whales experimenting with life in the ocean.

As I dug into the edge of a dry wash, I tried to visualize some of the varieties of whale ancestors that had been found here and nearby: Indocetus, Rodhocetus, Andrewsiphius, and Kutchicetus. No more than 5 to 15 feet long, they resembled big-headed, snaggle-toothed, web-footed sea lions or walruses and, like them, probably still returned to land to mate and give birth, schlumping along on ever punier hind legs. Yet analyses of oxygen isotopes in their teeth reveal that they no longer needed to drink fresh water as the walking, swimming whale did. These successors to Ambulocetus had crossed a crucial metabolic threshold on their way to becoming true marine mammals.

As the rear limbs dwindled, so did the hip bones that supported them. That made the spinal column more flexible to power the developing tail flukes. The neck shortened, turning the leading end of the body into more of a tubular hull to plow through the water

---

"Whales underwent the most dramatic and complete transformation of any mammal."—Hans Thewissen, Northeastern Ohio University, College of Medicine

---

with minimum drag, while the arms assumed the shape of rudders. Having little need for outer ears any longer, some whales were receiving waterborne sounds directly through their lower jawbones and transmitting them to the inner ears via special fat pads. Each whale in the sequence was a little more streamlined than earlier models and roamed farther from shore.

The makeover from landlubbers to seafarers happened in less than ten million years—overnight on the geologic time scale. As Thewissen put it, "Whales underwent the most dramatic and complete transformation of any mammal. The early stages were so poorly known 15 years ago that creationists held up whales as proof that species couldn't possibly have come about through natural selection. Now whales are one of the better examples of evolution."

Hoisting a partial skull I had just pried from sunstruck rubble, I trotted over to Bajpai. He said it belonged to an ancient whale named Remingtonocetus, identified by its long, narrow jaws. "We assume they were for snapping up fish, like the modern gharial crocodile does with its needle-like snout," he said. "It is a specialization that appears several times among later cetaceans, including modern river dolphins."

As temperatures shimmered toward 115°F, stories from Hindu mythology came and went in my overcooked brain. I contemplated siddhas, those who have the mystical power to assume any shape, fly over mountains, and even defy death. Sleeving sweat from my eyes, I thought: What's so supernatural about that? Life has found ways to flourish in boiling hot springs and on icy mountaintops, to fly, glow in the dark, put forth leaves in a rainless desert, or plumb the ocean, reproducing and adapting, reincarnating itself in new forms in defiance of time and death.

About 40 million years ago, as ancient whales spread out from the Tethys Sea, considered the cradle of whale evolution, a group known as the dorudontines arose. Although they could still bend their flippers at the elbow and their nostrils had moved only partway from the snout toward the top of the head, in most other respects these were full-fledged, fluke-lashing cetaceans that gave birth at sea. They may have been the dynasty that went on to produce modern whales. The giant serpent-like Basilosaurus, a contemporary, was surely a hunter to be reckoned with—the fossilized stomach contents I saw contained 13 kinds of fish and sharks up to three feet long.

James Goedert knows a lot about how lines diverge or connect. After all, he is a signal inspector for a railroad. Give him a day off and he and his wife, Gail, are questing after extinct whales. They've been at it 20 years, looking mostly in the epoch after the Eocene, the Oligocene, from 34 million to 24 million years ago.

"When we began," said Jim, also a part-time paleontologist for the Burke Museum at the University of Washington, "there were archaeocetes, or ancient whales, and then there were recognizable baleen and toothed whales. What came in between? The Oligocene, and it was pretty much a big blank. If you find a whale from this time period, chances are it's a new species or even a whole new family. And when I do find one, there's no feeling like it."

This is a man happy to prospect from dawn 'til dusk and return at night with a lantern, saying the play of shadows can catch hard-to-see bone outlines. The Goederts' efforts have produced the oldest odontocete, several of the earliest mysticetes, and the North Pacific's oldest whale.

We waded among tide pools on Washington's Olympic Peninsula for days. Had I looked out across the Strait of Juan de Fuca, I might have found live gray whales or killer whales. But if a fossil whale lay anywhere among the seaweed underfoot, I couldn't get my eye on it.

Jim's backpack was already loaded with skull remains. What we were doing, he said, was equivalent to traveling back countless lifetimes, proceeding miles out into the ocean, then dropping 6,000 to 9,000 feet below the surface to hike the seafloor until we came across sunken whale carcasses. Luckily, geologic forces had compressed those bottom sediments into stone and thrust them up to be pasted onto the continent's edge, after which rainstorms and waves eroded the seaward slopes, bringing fossils down onto the beaches. In short, the hard work had been done for us; he told me, keep looking.

Finally I found a fossil that didn't turn out to be a fish or burly Oligocene seabird. Jim said, "You're looking at a very primitive true toothed whale." Here was a link between the ancient whales, which each carried a mix of different-shaped teeth as a legacy of their days on land, and odontocetes (the division with sperm whales, dolphins, and their kin), whose teeth are more like uniform spear tips or pegs.

Perhaps the most important features in this transitional animal were associated with the skull's architecture: the beginnings of special sacs off the main nasal passage for moving air back and forth to create sound vibrations; a lens of fatty tissue, called the melon, in the forehead for focusing outgoing sounds; and thinned portions of the lower jaw to help catch returning vibrations. Together they added up to the ability to navigate and to find prey through echolocation, a key to the success of the toothed whale group.

Waving me over to the surf's edge, Jim pointed to a mineralized skeleton of an aetiocetid, a ten-foot-long beast that helped bridge the gap between the ancient whales and baleen whales. Call it one more missing link that is no longer missing, for the animal had teeth yet also showed signs it was developing baleen plates from skin tissue on a widened upper jaw. Modern baleen whales still grow teeth while in the womb but reabsorb them before birth. They don't need chompers anymore; their heads have become, in effect, living nets. The evolution of long strips of baleen did for them what sonar did for the toothed whales; it pushed their effectiveness as predators a quantum leap forward.

Lawrence Barnes, a paleontologist from the Natural History Museum of Los Angeles County, led me into the next epoch, the Miocene, which lasted from 24 to 5 million years ago, at a dig known as Sharktooth Hill near Bakersfield, California. Somebody got the name right; I no sooner sat down for a snack on chalky former seafloor than the fang of a shark lying in wait for eons reached out and bit me on the butt.

"The site has some 30 kinds of cetaceans, so the cast of characters was about as varied as a similar locale in modern times," Barnes said.

I joined museum volunteers shoveling and screening the sediments. Over the months and years, they had helped unearth eight species of baleen whales called cetotheres. Though relatively primitive, this line survived until three million years ago, coexisting with the modern family of bowheads and right whales, which first appeared 22 million years ago. One reason bowheads and right whales attain weights of 80 tons or more, Barnes explained, is that they have evolved the longest, most elaborate baleen of any whales and use it to comb swarms of abundant plankton from the seawater. Over time cetotheres were replaced by the family of sleek, faster moving rorquals, whose modern members include such behemoths as blue and sei whales. A different kind of feeding efficiency led to their tremendous size; pleats along a rorqual's underside allow its throat to expand like an accordion when gulping seawater teeming with food.

The diagram of the whale family tree remains far from finished.

In addition Sharktooth Hill has yielded two kinds of sperm whales and at least half a dozen kinds of primitive dolphins called kentriodontids, plus one of the earliest delphinoids, as members of the major family of modern dolphins are known. Back at the museum, Barnes brought out a dolphin skull to show me how the bones of the snout extend back over the brain case, a move related to the evolution of the fatty melon and air sacs that produce the sounds used in echolocation. In some species the forehead area even has a concavity like a small satellite dish, which may boost the animal's echolocation abilities.

The dolphin skull was a reminder that whale evolution has not necessarily been toward bigness. The sophisticated, talkative whales we label dolphins are the most varied and numerous of the cetaceans today. Fashion models outweigh the four-foot-long porpoises called vaquitas, now endangered in the Gulf of California.

From the Miocene onward, whales could take advantage of prey from tiny crustaceans and sardine schools to sea lions and giant squid, from the surface to the abyss. They had arrived. They had walked, waded, paddled, and fluked their way to dominion over most of the blue planet. At what stage did they come up with extra myoglobin in their muscles for storing oxygen on longer dives? When did humpbacks start singing one of the most elaborate, evocative songs ever heard? Because changes in physiology and behavior aren't always associated with obvious shifts in anatomy, they can be harder to track. We only know that when modern whales emerged they continued to refine their adaptations and prosper.

The diagram of the whale family tree remains far from finished. Many branches need to be filled in, and a revision has lately been suggested for the roots. Scientists have known since the 1880s that whales and ruminants both possess multichambered stomachs and a similar pattern of folding on the brain's cortex. Then modern molecular biologists began finding telltale matches of proteins and amino acids between whales and artiodactyls, hoofed animals with an even number of toes, which include ruminants as well as pigs and hippos. Yet, until recently, the hard evidence of fossil teeth and skull features seemed to tie whales to a different group of hoofed creatures, meat-eaters known as mesonychids. Now ankle bones from two new early whale species, discovered by Philip Gingerich of the University of Michigan and colleagues and described in a recent issue of the journal Science, point back to artiodactyl origins.

Norihiro Okada of the Tokyo Institute of Technology has no doubt whose picture would hang on the wall if whales kept portraits of their nearest living relatives. "Hippos," he declared at his lab in Japan. Okada and his colleagues have discovered unique genetic markers shared only by whales and hippos, indicating a common ancestor. "It is the solution to a problem that has continued more than a century," he said.

If Okada is right, it could mean that whales descended from a group of primitive artiodactyls called anthracotheres, modest-size beasts with a piggish appearance and four hoofed toes on each foot, as hippos have today. Abundant in Eurasia throughout the early age of mammals, the anthracotheres produced a number of marsh-dwelling forms.

Talking with Lawrence Barnes, I recalled my first sight of a dolphin from the Pliocene whose blunt nose, squarish head, and long tusks resembled a mollusk-eating walrus. The fossil made me wonder aloud how many varieties of whales had taken their turn upon life's stage. Barnes replied, "I've never added them up. Why don't you try?" and left me standing before his drawers of file cards representing the cetacean species identified by science. Hours later I told Barnes I had counted around a thousand. He said, "My guess is that represents 10 percent of what's out there waiting to be dug up." I know what Jim Goedert would say: Keep looking. The world holds more miracles—big, small, new, and old—than we can imagine.

Little Meat-Eater Is No Bird, but Close

By William Mullen
Chicago Tribune, October 13, 2005

A turkey-size, carnivorous dinosaur that looked something like a diminutive but malevolent version of Big Bird from "Sesame Street" is changing scientists' thinking about when and where some of the closest relatives to birds evolved.

Buitreraptor is named for La Buitrera, an area of the Patagonian desert in Argentina where paleontologists found an almost complete skeleton of the 90-million-year-old, probably feathered creature in January 2004. It is described in Thursday's issue of the science journal *Nature*.

The fossil buitreraptor (pronounced bwee-trey-rap-ter) conclusively proves that a family of small, swift dinosaurs called dromaeosaurs evolved tens of millions of years earlier than previously believed, said Field Museum paleontologist Peter Makovicky, the article's lead author.

Until now, scientists believed that dromaeosaurs—meat-eaters that include the famous velociraptor—evolved in the Northern Hemisphere after the world's land mass split into two supercontinents, Gondwanaland and Laurasia, 135 million years ago.

The presence of buitreraptor in South America proves dromaeosaurs evolved before that split—140 million to 145 million years ago—and spread throughout the world.

"We can now push the history of dromaeosaurs as far back as the first birds, like archaeopteryx," Makovicky said.

Close Relation to Birds

Buitreraptor and dinosaurs like it are not the ancestors of birds—they lived simultaneously—but they are closely related.

"Dromaeosaurs are really interesting because they are so close to birds in evolution, having feathers and other, similar attributes," said American Museum paleontologist Mark Norell, who called the work by Makovicky and two Argentine colleagues an important discovery.

Dromaeosaurs are a subgroup of theropods, two-legged carnivorous dinosaurs that also include Tyrannosaurus rex. Buitreraptor has the characteristic wishbone, birdlike pelvis and long, winglike forelimbs of a dromaeosaur.

"It is the most complete small theropod ever found in South America," said Makovicky.

Yet buitreraptor is also something of an odd duck. Its skull and jaws are more slender and less powerful than other known dromaeosaurs, and its relatively short teeth lack the sharp, serrated edges of most theropod teeth.

"Instead of powerful jaws, it relied more on being able to very quickly open and close its jaws," Makovicky said. "Other dromaeosaurs and theropods tended to feed on large prey, but this one seems to have eaten small prey, like rat-sized mammals that ran around then, and lizards and the primitive snakes of that time."

The fossil presents "a very neat evolutionary picture," Makovicky said, because the presence of dromaeosaurs shows how old that family of animals is, "how it was distributed, how the north and south branches of the family evolved differently in isolation."

Similar to China Fossils

Though the fossil was located in a type of rock formation that could not preserve evidence of feathers, Makovicky said he believed it almost certainly was feathered because of its similarities to two dromaeosaur fossils found in China, microraptor and sinornithosaurus. Those specimens were found in extremely fine limestone beds that preserved impressions of the animals' extensive plumage.

"It could not fly," Makovicky said of buitreraptor, "but it may have had some aerodynamic capability," perhaps being able to glide.

Prior to buitreraptor's discovery, paleontologists had found bone fragments of animals that some suspected were dromaeosaurs, but the finds were too incomplete to confirm it.

In 2003, Argentine paleontologist Sebastian Apesteguia found a bone sticking out of a rock cliff in Patagonia that he thought might be from a dromaeosaur. In 2004 he invited Makovicky, who specializes in carnivorous dinosaurs, to collaborate with him and another Argentine colleague, Federico Agnolin.

The fossil was embedded in rock so hard that they had to remove a 4-foot-long, half-foot-thick slab from the cliff so the bones could be chipped out in a laboratory. After preliminary work in Argentina, the final preparation was done at the Field Museum in Chicago.

The skeleton is back in Argentina, which owns it, but a replica is at the Field.

The Patagonian region in which it was found is rich with dinosaur fossils. Buitreraptor lived in a forested plain where it and other small animals shared the ecosystem with huge plant-eaters and T. rex–style predators, including the 45-foot-long giganotosaurus, a fossil of which was found 60 miles from the buitreraptor site in 1993.

Buried During Flooding

Buitreraptor and other small animals found near it probably died and were buried during seasonal flooding, said Makovicky.

"Those flood events would barely wash the ankles of the big dinosaurs in the forest," he said. But big animals like giganotosaurus could get caught and killed in deep, raging rivers in the region, with flood debris eventually preserving their bones in rock.

"This area of Patagonia is one of the only places in the world where the fossil record has both big and small fossil animals," said Makovicky. "They just aren't together. Each was fossilized in a different depositional mechanism that tended to sort out the size of animals.

"In terms of figuring out the ecosystem it is pretty nice."

The Astonishing Micropygmies

BY JARED DIAMOND
SCIENCE, DECEMBER 17, 2004

By now, every Science reader will have read about the discovery of skeletons representing a primitive human micropygmy population that survived until about 18,000 years ago on the Indonesian island of Flores [1,2] These creatures were barely 3 feet tall, and had an estimated body weight of 20 kg and a brain size of 380 cm³ (smaller than that of a chimpanzee). They seem to be more similar to Homo erectus than to Homo sapiens, and are thought to have descended from H. erectus independently of sapiens' descent from erectus. When I first learned of this discovery, I thought it the most astonishing in any field of science within the last decade. On reflection, paraphrasing Elizabeth Barrett Browning, let me count the ways in which it is (and is not) astonishing.

In situations like this one, I've found it useful to get the perspective of a green extraterrestrial friend visiting Earth from the Andromeda Nebula. My friend remarked, "Once again, you humans are prisoners of your ingrained species-centric biases. You already know that large mammals colonizing remote small islands tend to evolve into isolated populations of dwarfs. You have examples of insular pygmy hippos, buffalo, ground sloths, true elephants, stegodont elephants, mammoths, 'Irish' elk, red deer, and even dinosaurs. So, now you have 10 examples instead of 9. What's so astonishing? Since when aren't humans subject to natural selection?"

E.T.'s response forced me to reflect. One surprise, I realized, is that we're uncertain exactly which selective pressures do select for insular dwarfs. A favorite theory is ecological release from competition, when a big species reaches an island lacking the mainland suite of smaller related species. According to this argument, the Flores micropygmy would have evolved to occupy a niche of abundant food left vacant by the lack of native apes, monkeys, and other small flightless mammals (except for rodents and a dwarfed elephant) on this island. Another favorite theory is the supposed resource poverty of islands, such that small-bodied animals will be less likely to starve than large-bodied animals. At the level of individual selection, that argument won't work: Flores and other islands with dwarfed mammals have productivities per hectare at least as high as those of continents. But the argument could work at the level of group selection and could explain the regularly increasing relation between body mass of an island's or continent's top carnivore (or herbivore) and the area of the land mass [3]. What counts is the island's total productivity rather than its productivity per hectare: An isolated population of 100 full-sized human hunter-gatherers on Flores would have been at a much higher risk of extinction than an isolated population of 700 micropygmies.

E.T.'s blasé reaction then made me think further: Flores is just one of hundreds of islands in its size range, so why weren't there micropygmies on many other islands? The catch is that, for dwarfing to evolve on an island, you need humans just barely capable of reaching the island: If they could reach it too easily, the continuing arrival of full-sized colonists would prevent evolutionary divergence. Once modern H. sapiens developed the technology to reach islands, the resulting insular populations were constantly faced with new arrivals and were no longer isolated. Hence the only examples of effectively isolated insular sapiens populations known to me are from so-called land-bridge islands (like Britain and Japan) formerly connected to adjacent continents at Pleistocene times of low sea level, and isolated around 10,000 years ago when world ice sheets melted and sea levels rose. Some recent sapiens populations on those land-bridge islands were descended from ancestors who walked to the island during land-bridge times, lacked watercraft, and thus became completely isolated when the land bridge was severed.

For instance, the Australian land-bridge island of Tasmania is known to have supported a human population that survived in isolation for 10,000 years after Tasmania became cut off from Australia [4]. Tasmania was large enough that full-sized humans are predicted from regression equations [3] to have lived there—and modern Aboriginal Tasmanians were indeed full-sized. However, the much smaller Australian land-bridge island of Flinders supported a human population that succumbed to isolation only after about 4000 years [5]: I am unaware of skeletal remains that indicate whether these humans became reduced in size. Promising locations to search for erectus micropygmies are other Indonesian islands besides Flores: surely Lombok and Sumbawa, through which erectus colonists from the Asian mainland must have passed to reach Flores; and perhaps Sumba, Timor, Celebes, and others. My first bet is on Celebes.

How did the ancestors of the Flores micropygmies, whoever they were, reach Flores? At Pleistocene times of low sea level, the Indonesian island chain of the Greater Sunda Islands was connected to the Asian mainland as far east as Java and Bali, but water gaps of 6, 19, and 3 km, respectively, separated Bali from Penida, Penida from Lombok and Sumbawa (joined in the Pleistocene), and Lombok and Sumbawa from Flores and Lomblen (also joined in the Pleistocene) [6]. Across each of those water gaps, the island on the far side would have been visible to someone standing on the island on the near side. Hence the micropygmies' ancestors could have colonized the island by sailing toward it in a watercraft (perhaps a rudimentary raft, or a mere floating log), or they could have landed on the island accidentally when their watercraft was swept to sea by ocean currents. Perhaps they even swam to the island. Stegodont elephants reached Flores and Timor and Celebes, and monkeys and buffalo and squirrels also reached Celebes, all surely without making rafts; H. erectus presumably could have as well.

Why haven't remains of erectus-like humans been found in Australia and New Guinea, at the eastern end of the Indonesian island chain? Possibly, for the same reason they weren't found on Flores until 2004; perhaps these humans did reach Australia and New Guinea, but archaeologists just haven't looked hard enough for their remains. I doubt this answer; hundreds of Pleistocene human sites are now known in Australia, with no remains of humans other than those of sapiens. Instead, the answer probably has to do with geography. A modern map plus bathymetric charts show that, even at Pleistocene times of low sea level, a water gap of at least 87 km separated the easternmost Indonesian islands from either Australia or New Guinea, which would not have been visible across that wide gap [6]. Such gaps were too wide not only for pre-sapiens humans, but also for stegodonts, monkeys, buffalo, and squirrels, none of which are found in Australia and New Guinea.

The discoverers of the Flores micropygmies conclude that they survived on Flores until at least 18,000 years ago [1,2]. To me, that is the most astonishing finding, even more astonishing than the micropygmies' existence. We know that full-sized H. sapiens reached Australia and New Guinea through Indonesia by 46,000 years ago, that most of the large mammals of Australia then promptly went extinct (probably in part exterminated by H. sapiens), and that the first arrival of behaviorally modern H. sapiens on all other islands and continents in the world was accompanied by similar waves of extinction/extermination. We also know that humans have exterminated competing humans even more assiduously than they have exterminated large nonhuman mammals. How could the micropygmies have survived the onslaught of H. sapiens?

One could perhaps seek a parallel in the peaceful modern coexistence of full-sized sapiens and pygmy sapiens in the Congo and Philippines, based on complementary economies, with pygmy hunter-gatherers trading forest products to full-sized sapiens farmers. But full-sized sapiens hunter-gatherers 18,000 years ago would have been much too similar economically to micropygmy hunter-gatherers to permit coexistence based on complementary economies and trade. One could also invoke the continued coexist-

The discoverers of the Flores micropygmies conclude that they survived on Flores until at least 18,000 years ago.

ence of chimpanzees and humans in Africa, based on chimps being economically too different from us to compete (very doubtful for micropygmies), and on chimps being too dangerous to be worth hunting (probably true for micropygmies). Then, one could point to the reported survival of the pygmy stegodont elephants on Flores until 12,000 years ago [1, 2]: If stegodonts survived so long in the presence of H. sapiens, why not micropygmies as well? Finally, one might suggest that all of the recent dates for stegodonts and micropygmies on Flores are in error [despite the evidence presented in [1] and [2]], and that both stegodonts and micropygmies became extinct 46,000 years ago within a century of H. sapiens' arrival on Flores. All of these analogies and suggestions strike me as implausible: I just can't conceive of a long temporal overlap of sapiens and erectus, and I am reluctant to believe that all of the dates in [1] and [2] are wrong. Hence I don't know what to make of the reported coexistence.

At last comes the question that all of us full-sized sapiens wanted to ask but didn't dare: Did full-sized sapiens have sex with micropygmies? The difference in body size would not have been an insuperable obstacle: Some individual modern humans have sex with children or with domestic animals no larger than the micropygmies. I suspect that the answer is the same as the answer to the question of whether we modern humans have sex with chimpanzees. We don't, because chimps are too unlike humans to appeal sexually to most of us, and because chimps are much too strong, unpredictable, and dangerous to make sex a safe proposition for any individual humans who might find them sexually attractive. Ditto for H. erectus, even when dwarfed.

References:

1. P. Brown et al., Nature 431, 1055 (2004).

2. M. J. Morwood et al., Nature 431, 1087 (2004).

3. G. P. Burness, J. Diamond, T. Flannery, Proc. Natl. Acad. Sci. U.S.A. 98, 14518 (2001).

4. R. Jones, in Sunda and Sahul, J. Allen, J. Golson, R. Jones, Eds. (Academic Press, London, 1977), pp. 317–386.

5. R. Sim, in Archaeology in the North, M. Sullivan, S. Brockwell, A. Webb, Eds. (North Australia Research Unit, Darwin, 1994), pp. 358–374.

6. J. Birdsell, in Sunda and Sahul, J. Allen, J. Golson, R. Jones, Eds. (Academic Press, London, 1977), pp. 113–167.

V. Cognition and Culture

Editors' Introduction

The theory of evolution has ruffled feathers not only because it contradicts a literal reading of the book of Genesis but also because it undermines the primacy of the human species: in evolutionary terms, we are just another animal, another form of primate. Such a notion does not sit well with those who are accustomed to seeing the world as constructed for man.[1] Although human beings have transformed the environment of this planet to an extent that no other animal has, it has become increasingly apparent that higher cognition and culture are not the sole provinces of humanity. Through the work of such noted primatologists as Jane Goodall, Dian Fossey, and Frans de Waal, it is now known that great apes are capable of such complex feats as toolmaking and forming political alliances.

Simon M. Reader, in his article "Don't Call Me Clever," explains that while it might be tempting when examining the complexities of human intelligence to rank it among the pinnacles of evolution, our intellectual abilities have drawbacks as well. Biologists have long struggled to explain how and why intelligent behavior evolved among some species, and most scientists seem to agree that the ability to learn benefits species that live in highly variable environments. Measuring the intelligence of other species presents another problem. Chimpanzees—our nearest living relative, next to bonobos—do learn from one another but not as easily as humans do.

Chimps and other great apes, however, do share an intellectual skill with humans (and possibly dolphins) that is rare in the animal kingdom: They are able to recognize themselves in their reflections. As Nicholas Wade explains in "Who's That Strange Monkey in the Mirror? A Tufted Capuchin Isn't Quite Sure," this ability was once thought to "mark a bright line between these species and monkeys," but research recently conducted by Frans de Waal indicates that the monkey's mental processes may be more complicated than was initially assumed.

Based on archaeological remains left by Ice Age Europeans, anthropologists once believed that the emergence of the modern human mind—that is, an intelligence similar to ours—occurred 40,000 years ago, when *Homo sapiens* abruptly began producing art, music, and advanced weaponry. But, as Kate Wong details in "The Morning of the Modern Mind," a growing number of archaeologists have begun to question the "big bang theories of the origin of culture," pointing to recently unearthed evidence of cultural sophistication from African sites.

---

[1] See Mark Twain's satirical essay on this topic, "Was the World Made for Man?" in the appendix of this book.

Archaeologists also debate how long humans and their ancestors have practiced the cultural innovation of cooking. In "Early Chefs Left Indelible Mark on Human Evolution," James Randerson explains the work of a team of anthropologists who claim that *Homo erectus*—a species that sported the largest increase in human brain size on record—must have cooked its food in order to obtain the protein needed to support such a large brain.

The origins of another cultural adaptation, singing, also confounds biologists: though they have been unable to identify exactly how the ability to sing would have helped humans to survive, neurological evidence suggests that it is not merely a side effect of the development of intelligence and language. In "Caveman Crooners," Sharon Begley discusses the theory that music helped develop a social identity among our ancestors.

Don't Call Me Clever

BY SIMON M. READER
NEW SCIENTIST, JULY 17–23, 2004

At first glance, Homo sapiens seems an unlikely candidate for world domination. Our bodies are puny and defenceless, with none of the obvious trappings of a top predator. But no matter, the secret of our success is measured not in brawn but in brains. That makes it tempting to rate the creativity and complex learning abilities that characterise human intelligence as the pinnacle of evolution. Tempting, but wrong.

Think about it. If our kind of intelligence is such a good thing, why is it unique in nature? Given around 3.8 billion years of evolution since life began, you might expect other organisms to have come up with the same winning formula. Yet our big brains are the exception, not the rule. Most animals get by perfectly well with tiny brains and apparently limited learning abilities. Perhaps the combination of a large brain and advanced intelligence isn't a universal winning ticket in the evolution lottery, but is instead just another evolutionary adaptation.

This perspective raises some key questions. What is intelligence good for and, more importantly, what is it bad for? Are humans unique in having taken an evolutionary path that emphasises intelligent behaviour, or have other animals taken a similar route? How do we know which animals are smarter than others, anyway? One surprising conclusion is that, often, it pays to have limited intelligence. Another is that where intelligence has evolved it may have been driven by struggling losers rather than successful individuals.

Advanced learning skills form a fundamental part of what we term intelligent behaviour. Superior learning abilities may initially appear unquestionably useful, but this is far from a universal truth. Animals that instinctively know which predators to avoid, which foods to eat, or what their mother looks like, are less vulnerable than those that have to learn such skills. Learning takes time, and you risk making mistakes: if you happen to be looking at a flower while everybody else is freaking out over a snake, you could end up with a mistaken fear of tulips. Still, many animals, from fish to monkeys, do learn about potential sources of danger from others. But they usually have in-built predispositions that influence the kinds of things they can learn. Rhesus macaques, for example, learn from other macaques to fear snakes more readily than flowers.

But other costs of learning are unavoidable. Brain tissue is among the most energy-hungry of all body tissues. Around 20 per cent of your resting metabolism goes to supplying the energy demands of your brain, compared with 3 per cent in a typical smaller-brained mammal. Then there's the cost of protecting this sensitive structure from mechanical and physiological shocks, which means a thick skull, specialised temperature regulation, and adaptations for precisely controlling the brain's chemical environment. Larger brains also take longer to develop, so parents must invest additional time and energy in gestating and raising each offspring. All this means larger-brained animals could be at a substantial reproductive disadvantage compared with their smaller-brained counterparts.

> *Natural selection will ensure that increased intelligence evolves only in those species where the total benefits outweigh the costs.*

Proving this experimentally is difficult, but one recent study provides a fascinating insight into why many species remain less intelligent. Frederic Mery and Tadeusz Kawecki at the University of Fribourg in Switzerland were able to breed a strain of fruit flies that was smarter than average. To do this, the insects were allowed to feed on orange and pineapple-flavoured jellies, one of which contained bitter-tasting quinine. Later, the flies could choose to lay their eggs on either flavour jelly—both now without the bitter taste—but only eggs laid on the flavour that was not previously tainted were allowed to develop into adults. With each subsequent generation, the researchers switched the flavour containing the bitter taste, to ensure that they were selecting flies with better memories rather than a preference for a particular jelly flavour.

They found that within 20 generations their flies had better learning abilities than control flies on a variety of tasks. But the clever individuals weren't some kind of super-fly: in domains other than learning their more stupid cousins had the upper hand. For example, larvae of flies bred for cleverness did worse than those of regular flies when competing for limited food (Proceedings of the Royal Society of London, vol 270, p 2465).

Clearly the lab is an artificial environment for fruit flies, and the costs and benefits of intelligence will be different in the wild, but this experiment reveals that while improved learning capacities may increase an individual's survival chances in one arena, it can reduce them in others. Natural selection will ensure that increased intelligence evolves only in those species where the total benefits outweigh the costs.

Ever since Darwin, biologists have been interested in what kinds of species demonstrate intelligent behaviour, and why. The consensus is that environmental variability is the key. Mathematical models such as those developed by Peter Richerson from the University of California, Davis, and Robert Boyd from the University of California, Los Angeles, reveal that when the environment is changing slowly, an organism's best option is genetically encoded stock responses. However, as the environment changes more rapidly, learning becomes a better strategy for survival. At intermediate rates of change, the ideal tactic is learning from others—social learning. At more rapid rates, individual learning works best.

Different theories and different researchers emphasise different aspects of environmental variability to explain the evolution of intelligence. Social-intelligence hypotheses focus on the benefits of braininess in dealing with a rapidly changing social world. They argue that intelligence helps individuals cope with the demands of social living, allowing them to gain information from others to behave unpredictably—which may be key in outwitting rivals. Thus clever individuals may not only cope better with variability, but may actively create variability in their own behaviour. And research shows that mammals living in larger social groups—who must presumably keep track of more individuals and relationships—do have larger brains than less social species, relative to their body size.

As the environment changes more rapidly, learning becomes a better strategy for survival.

Other biologists focus more on the demands of tracking changes in the physical environment, such as the distribution of food, or the need to learn how to access hard-to-eat foods. Supporters of "ecological intelligence" theories point out that species eating foods that are patchily distributed in space and time—such as fruit—have bigger brains than those that eat more dependable, widespread foods such as leaves.

Then there are researchers who suggest that intelligence evolves as a result of positive feedback. They propose that more intelligent species tend to expose themselves to more variable environmental situations where learning is advantageous—eating novel—for example—which in turn creates selection pressure for even better learning abilities. However, whales and dolphins present a problem for this theory. Until two million years ago cetaceans had the biggest brains of all mammals—even taking their body size into account—yet their brain volumes have grown little in the past 15 million years.

All these theories invoke natural selection, but it may not be the only force at work. Some people argue that cognitive abilities have less to do with increasing survival and more to do with attracting or choosing mates—sexual selection. The thinking goes that because brains are complex, costly structures, potential mates may view high intelligence as an indicator of a high-quality individual. This might explain why some male songbirds have such an extensive vocal repertoire, for instance.

Geoffrey Miller of the University of New Mexico in Albuquerque has used a similar argument to explain human intelligence. If generations of our ancestors preferred to mate with innovative and creative individuals, this would have shaped the evolution of our brains in much the same way that the peahen's preferences have shaped the peacock's tail. There is evidence that sexual selection has produced larger brains in some bowerbirds but its part in the evolution of human brains remains firmly at the nice-idea stage.

Nevertheless, all this theorising suggests that there are a variety of reasons why some species might find that the benefits of evolving big, intelligent brains outweigh the costs. In our own species this process has led to a particular kind of learning strategy, characterised by creativity and cultural transmission—the spread of ideas and know-how from person to person. We humans are innovators par excellence, rivalling evolution's powers of invention by at least one yardstick: the number of registered patents outnumbers the living species that have been discovered. We also have an outstanding cultural diversity. What's more, we are especially good at learning from one another, and think nothing of feats such as learning by imitation, which even our closest relative the chimpanzee struggles to do.

So how unique is our kind of intelligence? Experiments with chimps and other higher primates reveal exciting, albeit controversial, parallels with human cognition. But comparing the mental abilities of animals as varied as ants, albatrosses and aardvarks is even more tricky. Obviously you can measure brain size, but are animals with large brains actually more intelligent? We routinely use words like "brainy" as synonyms for intelligence, and even animal behaviourists have assumed they equate, but in fact we have only recently been able to confirm that bigger brains do indeed provide superior cognitive abilities. Even now, controversy rages over why big brains should be better. Meanwhile we have struggled to find a fair test to compare the cognitive abilities of a wide range of species, but recent years have seen a breakthrough. A growing number of researchers, including myself, have been focusing on innovation—the invention of novel behaviour patterns—as a measure of species' cognitive differences in one of the most human of all intellectual abilities, creativity.

This line of enquiry took off about seven years ago when Louis Lefebvre at McGill University in Montreal, Canada, realised that he could plunder the many publications devoted to birdwatching to glean comprehensive and reliable information about innovation in birds. Kevin Laland from the University of St Andrews in Scotland and I made a similar study of 116 primate species, also using published scientific reports of individuals' novel behaviour as an index of innovativeness. Both studies found that those animals with the largest brains relative to their body size were also the most innovative (Brain, Behavior and Evolution, vol 63, p 233). Thus it seems that for at least one measure of intelligence—innovativeness—there is indeed a link between brain volume and cognitive capacity.

These studies of innovation give us an unusual insight into the behaviour of a wide variety of animals in the wild. They can also provide clues to the evolutionary benefits and repercussions of innovative minds. In an intriguing follow-up to Lefebvre's work, Daniel Sol, now at the University of Barcelona in Spain, again took advantage of the fantastic record-keeping of bird enthusiasts to investigate how innovation affects survival. He looked at the 100-plus species of birds that human immigrants had introduced into New Zealand, often in deliberate attempts to recreate the fauna of their homeland. Combining detailed data on the success of these introduced species with Lefebvre's avian innovation database, Sol found species that were innovative in their original habitat were more likely to survive in New Zealand. For these birds at least, innovativeness seems to have helped in the struggle to cope with a new environment.

Studies of innovation reveal a wide range of creative ability in the animal world.

Even more noteworthy is the finding by Lefebvre and colleagues that innovation may affect the evolutionary process itself, with innovative lines of birds evolving more rapidly than less inventive lineages (Animal Behaviour, vol 65, p 445).

Studies of innovation reveal a wide range of creative ability in the animal world. While a monkey eating a new kind of root hardly seems to be making a cognitive leap, chimpanzees that create novel and highly effective courtship displays, such as flipping their upper lips over their noses, are more impressive. And top marks must surely go to Betty the New Caledonian crow who, when faced with a food basket at the bottom of a plastic tube, bent a piece of wire to make a hook-shaped tool to access the food: a novel solution to a novel problem (New Scientist, 17 August 2002, p 44).

But does even Betty demonstrate the same kind of creativity involved in human innovation? This question remains difficult to answer because we have only a rudimentary understanding of the mental processes involved. Many cases of innovation—including human creativity—can be explained in terms of simple trial-and-error learning, without the need for special cognitive skills, although Betty's achievements would be difficult to explain in these terms. The next challenge is to determine what is going on inside innovative minds, both human and animal, so we can see exactly what makes human creativity so special.

In one way, at least, the creative talents of animals do seem to mirror those of humans. In those animals examined up to now the adage "necessity is the mother of invention" rings true. My own experiments with guppies reveal that hungry, small and uncompetitive fish tend to be the most innovative. And among primates, innovators are usually individuals of low social rank. In humans too, innovation is often used only when things are going badly. Businesses and individuals both tend to stick to tried-and-tested formulas if they can.

If inventiveness were indeed a universal panacea, this reluctance to use it might seem bizarre. But once you understand that intelligence is just another survival strategy, it makes more sense. Innovation may provide benefits, such as novel food sources or more efficient foraging techniques, but it also carries costs—the risk of poisoning or the energy wasted trying something new that doesn't work out. In humans, pursuing innovation at the wrong time has led to numerous bankruptcies and even death. So we should expect those animals using their full creative potential to be either individuals who can afford to bear the potential costs of their experimentation or those in such dire need that they are turning to innovation as a last resort. It's a high-risk strategy, but if the gamble pays off they might just hit the evolutionary jackpot.

In other words, the story of the evolution of human creative intelligence is perhaps not one of successful individuals innovating to do still better, but rather one of losers innovating to do less badly.

Who's That Strange Monkey in the Mirror?

A Tufted Capuchin Isn't Quite Sure

BY NICHOLAS WADE
THE NEW YORK TIMES, JULY 26, 2005

Humans, the great apes and, probably, dolphins share an intellectual skill unusual in the animal world: they recognize their own reflections in a mirror.

That ability seems to mark a bright line between these species and monkeys, who, scientists have long assumed, look into mirrors and see only strangers. But a monkey's reaction to its reflection is more complex than is generally assumed, said Frans de Waal of the Yerkes National Primate Research Center in Atlanta.

Dr. de Waal and his colleagues were able to test the widely held belief that monkeys see strangers in the mirror using two troops of tufted capuchin monkeys at the Yerkes Center that had never met each other.

The capuchins, the Yerkes team is reporting today, understood at once that the mirror image was not a stranger, even though they failed to recognize themselves in the image. The findings appeared last week in The Proceedings of the National Academy of Sciences.

The female capuchins, the researchers found, avoided eye contact with a strange monkey while also making friendly overtures. But in front of a mirror their behavior was different. They looked often at their image, almost as if trying to flirt with it.

The male capuchins, in contrast, were seriously bothered by their image. Unlike Narcissus, they "appeared confused and distraught by their reflections" and often tried to escape from the testing room, the Yerkes team reports.

So what is going on in the monkeys' minds?

One possibility is that the image in the mirror is assigned to a mental category of "Puzzling Other," the researchers say. The male capuchins, particularly the high-ranking ones, may be discomfited by their reflection because it fails to play by the rules of the monkey hierarchy and show them due deference. On the other hand, this realization might be expected to build up gradually in the minds of the male monkeys, making it hard to explain why they instantly perceive that the image is not a stranger.

Human infants learn to recognize themselves in a mirror at 18 to 24 months, but they acquire an understanding of mirrors before that. Give a female chimp a mirror, and one can have no doubt she knows just what it is for.

The chimp will look at the two important parts of her body that she can usually never see, Dr. de Waal said. One is the inside of her mouth; the other is her rear end.

Mirror self-recognition is often regarded as a touchstone of self-awareness. But every animal must have some sense of self, for example in calculating its weight when grasping or sitting on thin branches.

Self-recognition, Dr. de Waal said, may tap into a higher sense of self. But there also may be a spectrum of self-awareness, with the capuchin's version falling short of the chimp's but above that of species that fail to recognize themselves. For example, the capuchin's understanding of mirrors is more advanced than that of male robins, who will ceaselessly attack the intruding male they see reflected, or that of cats and dogs, which will ignore a mirror once they have established there is nothing behind it.

Male capuchins probably react differently from females because they take their mirror image more seriously and don't know how to handle it, Dr. de Waal said. But both sexes seem to possess a greater understanding of the illusory qualities of mirrors than is generally assumed.

The Morning of the Modern Mind

By Kate Wong
Scientific American, June 2005

Christopher Henshilwood empties a tiny plastic bag and hands me a square of worn blue cardstock to which 19 snail shells no larger than kernels of corn have been affixed in three horizontal rows. To the casual onlooker, they might well appear unremarkable, a handful of discarded mollusk armor, dull and gray with age. In fact, they may be more precious than the glittering contents of any velvet-lined Cartier case.

The shells, discovered in a cave called Blombos located 200 miles east of here [Cape Town, South Africa], are perfectly matched in size, and each bears a hole in the same spot opposite the mouth, notes Henshilwood, an archaeologist at the University of Bergen in Norway. He believes they were collected and perforated by humans nearly 75,000 years ago to create a strand of lustrous, pearllike beads. If he is correct, these modest shells are humanity's crown jewels—the oldest unequivocal evidence of personal adornment to date and proof that our ancestors were thinking like us far earlier than is widely accepted.

A Behavioral Big Bang

By most accounts, the origin of anatomically modern *Homo sapiens* was a singularly African affair. In 2003 the unveiling of fossils found in Herto, Ethiopia, revealed that this emergence had occurred by 160,000 years ago. And in February 2005 researchers announced that they had redated *H. sapiens* remains from another Ethiopian site, Omo Kibish, potentially pushing the origin of our species back to 195,000 years ago.

Far less clear is when our kind became modern of mind. For the past two decades, the prevailing view has been that humanity underwent a behavioral revolution around 40,000 years ago. Scholars based this assessment primarily on the well-known cultural remains of Ice Age Europeans. In Europe, the relevant archaeological record is divided into the Middle Paleolithic (prior to around 40,000 years ago) and the Upper Paleolithic (from roughly 40,000 years ago onward), and the difference between the two could not be more striking. Middle Paleolithic people seem to have made mostly the same relatively simple stone tools humans had been producing for tens of thousands of years and not much else. The Upper Paleolithic, in contrast, ushered in a suite of sophisticated practices. Within a geologic blink of an eye, humans from the Rhône Valley to the Russian plain were producing advanced weaponry, forming long-distance trade networks, expressing themselves through art and music, and generally engaging in all manner of activities that archaeologists typically associate with modernity. It was, by all appearances, the ultimate Great Leap Forward.

Perhaps not coincidentally, it is during this Middle to Upper Paleolithic transition that humans of modern appearance had begun staking their claim on Europe, which until this point was strictly Neandertal territory. Although the identity of the makers of the earliest Upper Paleolithic artifacts is not known with certainty, because of a lack of human remains at the sites, they are traditionally assumed to have been anatomically modern *H. sapiens* rather than Neandertals. Some researchers have thus surmised that confrontation between the two populations awakened in the invaders a creative ability that had heretofore lain dormant.

Other specialists argue that the cultural explosion evident in Europe grew out of a shift that occurred somewhat earlier in Africa. Richard G. Klein of Stanford University, for one, contends that the abrupt change from the Middle to the Upper Paleolithic mirrors a transition that took place 5,000 to 10,000 years beforehand in Africa, where the comparative culture periods are termed the Middle and Later Stone Age. The impetus for this change, he theorizes, was not an encounter with another hominid type (for by this time in Africa, *H. sapiens* was free of competition with other human species) but rather a genetic mutation some 50,000 years ago that altered neural processes and thereby unleashed our forebears' powers of innovation.

Key evidence for this model, Klein says, comes from a site in central Kenya called Enkapune Ya Muto, the "twilight cave," that places the origin of the Later Stone Age at 45,000 to 50,000 years ago. There Stanley H. Ambrose of the University of Illinois and his team have uncovered obsidian knives, thumbnail-size scrapers and—most notably—tiny disk-shaped beads fashioned from ostrich eggshell in Later Stone Age levels dating back some 43,000 years. Strands of similar beads are still exchanged as gifts today among the !Kung San hunter-gatherers of Botswana. Ambrose posits that the ancient bead makers at Enkapune Ya Muto created them for the same reason: to foster good relationships with other groups as a hedge against hard times. If so, according to Klein, a genetically conferred ability to communicate through symbols—in concert with the cognitive prowess to conceive of better hunting technology and resource use—may have been what enabled our species finally, nearly 150,000 years after it originated, to set forth from its mother continent and conquer the world.

Seeds of Change

In recent years, however, a small but growing number of archaeologists have eschewed the big bang theories of the origin of culture in favor of a fundamentally different model. Proponents believe that there was no lag between body and brain. Rather, they contend, modern human behavior emerged over a long period in a process more aptly described as evolution than revolution. And some workers believe that cognitive modernity may have evolved in other species, such as the Neandertals, as well.

The notion that our species' peerless creativity might have primeval roots is not new. For years, scientists have known of a handful of objects that, taken at face value, suggest that humans were engaging in modern practices long before *H. sapiens* first painted a cave wall in France. They include three 400,000-year-old wooden throwing spears from Schöningen in Germany; a 233,000-year-old putative figurine from the site of Berekhat Ram in Israel; a 60,000-year-old piece of flint incised with concentric arcs from

---

A small but growing number of archaeologists have eschewed the big bang theories of the origin of culture in favor of a fundamentally different model.

Quneitra in Israel; two 100,000-year-old fragments of notched bone from South Africa's Klasies River Mouth Cave; and a polished plate of mammoth tooth from Tata in Hungary, dated to between 50,000 and 100,000 years ago. Many archaeologists looked askance at these remains, however, noting that their age was uncertain or that their significance was unclear. Any sign of advanced intellect that did seem legitimately ancient was explained away as a one-off accomplishment, the work of a genius among average Joes.

That position has become harder to defend in the face of the growing body of evidence in Africa that our forebears' mental metamorphosis began well before the start of the Later Stone Age. In a paper entitled "The Revolution That Wasn't: A New Interpretation of the Origin of Modern Human Behavior," published in the *Journal of Human Evolution* in 2000, Sally McBrearty of the University of Connecticut and Alison S. Brooks of George Washington University laid out their case. Many of the components of modern human behavior said to emerge in lockstep between 40,000 and 50,000 years ago, they argued, are visible tens of thousands of years earlier at Middle Stone Age locales. Moreover, they appear not as a package but piecemeal, at sites far-flung in time and space.

At three sites in Katanda in the Democratic Republic of the Congo, Brooks and John Yellen of the Smithsonian Institution have found elaborate barbed harpoons carved from bone that they say date to at least 80,000 years ago, which would place them firmly within the Middle Stone Age. These artifacts exhibit a level of sophistication comparable to that seen in 25,000-year-old harpoons from Europe, not only in terms of the complexity of the weapon design but the choice of raw material: the use of bone and ivory in tool manufacture was not thought to have occurred until the Later Stone Age and Upper Paleolithic. In addition, remains of giant Nile catfish have turned up with some of the Katanda harpoons, suggesting to the excavators that people were going there when the fish were spawning—the kind of seasonal mapping of resources previously thought to characterize only later humans.

> *Some discoveries hint that certain alleged aspects of behavioral modernity arose even before the genesis of* H. sapiens.

Other Middle Stone Age sites, such as ≠Gi (the "≠" denotes a click sound) in Botswana's Kalahari Desert, which is dated to 77,000 years ago, have yielded butchered animal remains that have put paid to another oft-made claim, namely, that these ancient people were not as competent at hunting as Later Stone Age folks. The residents at ≠Gi appear to have regularly pursued such large and dangerous prey as zebra and Cape warthog. And Hilary J. Deacon of Stellenbosch University has suggested that at sites such as South Africa's Klasies River Mouth Cave humans more than 60,000 years ago were deliberately burning grassland to encourage the growth of nutritious tubers, which are known to germinate after exposure to fire.

Some discoveries hint that certain alleged aspects of behavioral modernity arose even before the genesis of *H. sapiens*. Excavations in mid-2004 by McBrearty's team at a site near Lake Baringo in Kenya turned up stone blades—once a hallmark of the Upper Paleolithic material cultures—more than 510,000 years old. At a nearby locality, in levels dated to at least 285,000 years ago, her team has uncovered vast quantities of red ochre (a form of iron ore) and grindstones for processing it, signaling to McBrearty that the Middle Stone Age people at Baringo were using the pigment for symbolic purposes—to decorate their bodies, for instance—just as many humans do today. (Baringo is not the only site to furnish startlingly ancient evidence of ochre processing—Twin Rivers Cave in Zambia has yielded similar material dating back to more than 200,000 years ago.) And 130,000-year-old tool assemblages from Mumba Rock Shelter in Tanzania include flakes crafted from obsidian that came from a volcanic flow about 200 miles away—compelling evidence that the hominids who made the implements traded with other groups for the exotic raw material.

Critics, however, have dismissed these finds on the basis of uncertainties surrounding, in some cases, the dating and, in others, the intent of the makers. Ochre, for one, may have been used as mastic for attaching blades to wooden handles or as an antimicrobial agent for treating animal hides, skeptics note.

Smart for Their Age

It is against this backdrop of long-standing controversy that the discoveries at Blombos Cave have come to light. Henshilwood discovered the archaeological deposits at Blombos Cave in 1991 while looking for much younger coastal hunter-gatherer sites to excavate for his Ph.D. Located near the town of Still Bay in South Africa's southern Cape, on a bluff overlooking the Indian Ocean, the cave contained few of the Holocene artifacts he was looking for but appeared rich in Middle Stone Age material. As such, it was beyond the scope of his research at the time. In 1997, however, he raised the money to return to Blombos to begin excavating in earnest. Since then, Henshilwood and his team have unearthed an astonishing assemblage of sophisticated tools and symbolic objects and in so doing have sketched a portrait of a long-ago people who thought like us.

From levels dated by several methods to 75,000 years ago have come an array of advanced implements, including 40 bone tools, several of which are finely worked awls, and hundreds of bifacial points made of silcrete and other difficult-to-shape stones, which the Blombos people could have used to hunt the antelopes and other game that roamed the area. Some of the points are just an inch long, suggesting that they may have been employed as projectiles. And the bones of various species of deep-sea fish—the oldest of which may be more than 130,000 years old—reveal that the Blombos people had the equipment required to harvest creatures in excess of 80 pounds from the ocean.

Hearths for cooking indicate that the cave was a living site, and teeth representing both adults and children reveal that a family group dwelled there. But there are so many of the stone points, and such a range in their quality, that Henshilwood wonders whether the occupants may have also had a workshop in the tiny cave, wherein masters taught youngsters how to make the tools.

They may have passed along other traditions as well. The most spectacular material to emerge from Blombos is that which demonstrates that its occupants thought symbolically. By 2005 the team had recovered one piece of incised bone, nine slabs of potentially engraved red ochre and dozens of the tiny beads—all from the same 75,000-year-old layers that yielded the tools. In addition, sediments that may date back to more than 130,000 years ago contain vast quantities of processed ochre, some in crayon form.

Scientists may never know exactly what meaning the enigmatic etchings held for their makers. But it is clear that they were important to them. Painstaking analyses of two of the engraved ochres, led by Francesco d'Errico of the University of Bordeaux in France, have revealed that the rust-colored rocks were hand-ground on one side to produce a facet that was then etched repeatedly with a stone point. On the largest ochre, bold lines frame and divide the cross-hatched design.

Bead manufacture was likewise labor-intensive. Henshilwood believes the marine tick shells, which belong to the *Nassarius kraussianus* snail, were collected from either of two estuaries, located 12 miles from the cave, that still exist today. Writing in the January 2005 issue of the *Journal of Human Evolution*, Henshilwood, d'Errico and their colleagues report that experimental reconstruction of the process by which the shells were perforated indicates that the precocious jewelers used bone points to punch through the lip of the shell from the inside out—a technique that commonly broke the shells when attempted by team members. Once pierced, the beads appear to have been strung, as evidenced by the wear facets ringing the perforations, and traces of red ochre on the shells hint that they may have lain against skin painted with the pigment.

In the case for cognitive sophistication in the Middle Stone Age, "Blombos is the smoking gun," McBrearty declares. But Henshilwood has not convinced everyone of his interpretation. Doubts have come from Randall White of New York University, an expert on Upper Paleolithic body ornaments. He suspects that the perforations and apparent wear facets on the *Nassarius* shells are the result of natural processes, not human handiwork.

Overview/Evolved Thinking

- Archaeologists have traditionally envisioned *Homo sapiens* becoming modern of mind quickly and recently—sometime in the past 50,000 years, more than 100,000 years after attaining anatomical modernity.

- New discoveries in Africa indicate that many of the elements of modern human behavior can be traced much farther back in time.

- The finds suggest that our species had a keen intellect at its inception and exploited that creativity in archaeologically visible ways only when it was advantageous to do so—when population size increased, for instance.

- *H. sapiens* may not have been the only hominid to possess such advanced cognition: some artifacts hint that Neandertals were comparably gifted.

Here Today, Gone Tomorrow

If read correctly, however, the remarkable discoveries at Blombos offer weighty evidence that at least one group of humans possessed a modern mind-set long before 50,000 years ago, which may in some ways make previous claims for early behavioral modernity easier to swallow. So, too, may recent finds from sites such as Diep-kloof in South Africa's Western Cape, which has produced pieces of incised ostrich eggshell dated to around 60,000 years ago, and Loiyangalani in Tanzania, where workers have found ostrich egg-shell beads estimated to be on the order of 70,000 years old.

Yet it remains the case that most Middle Stone Age sites show few or none of the traits researchers use to identify fully developed cognition in the archaeological record. Several other locales in South Africa, for example, have yielded the sophisticated bifacial points but no evidence of symbolic behavior. Of course, absence of evidence is not evidence of absence, as prehistorians are fond of saying. It is possible the people who lived at these sites did make art and decorate their bodies, but only their stone implements have survived.

Perhaps the pattern evident thus far in the African record—that of ephemeral glimpses of cognitive modernity before the start of the Later Stone Age and ubiquitous indications of it after that—is just an artifact of preservational bias or the relatively small num-ber of African sites excavated so far. Then again, maybe these fits and starts are exactly what archaeologists should expect to see if anatomically modern *H. sapiens* possessed the capacity for modern human behavior from the get-go but tapped that potential only when it provided an advantage, as many gradualists believe.

The circumstances most likely to elicit advanced cultural behav-iors, McBrearty and others hypothesize, were those related to increased population size. The presence of more people put more pressure on resources, forcing our ancestors to devise cleverer ways to obtain food and materials for tool-making, she submits. More people also raised the chances of encounters among groups. Beads, body paint and even stylized tool manufacture may have functioned as indicators of an individual's membership and status in a clan, which would have been especially important when laying claim to resources in short supply. Symbolic objects may have also served as a social lubricant during stressful times, as has been argued for the beads from Enkapune Ya Muto.

"You have to make good with, groups around you because that's how you're going to get partners," Henshilwood observes. "If a gift exchange system is going on, that's how you're maintaining good relations." Indeed, gift giving may explain why some of the tools at Blombos are so aesthetically refined. A beautiful tool is not going to be a better weapon, he remarks, it is going to function as a sym-bolic artifact, a keeper of the peace.

Conversely, when the population dwindled, these advanced practices subsided—perhaps because the people who engaged in them died out or because in the absence of competition they simply did not pay off and were therefore forgotten. The Tasmanians provide a recent example of this relationship: when Europeans arrived in the region in the 17th century, they encountered a people whose material culture was simpler than even those of the Middle Paleolithic, consisting of little more than basic stone flake tools. Indeed, from an archaeological standpoint, these remains would have failed nearly all tests of modernity that are commonly applied to prehistoric sites. Yet the record shows that several thousand years ago, the Tasmanians possessed a much more complex tool kit, one that included bone tools, fishing nets, and bows and arrows. It seems that early Tasmanians had all the latest gadgetry before rising sea levels cut the island off from the mainland 10,000 years ago but lost the technology over the course of their small group's separation from the much larger Aboriginal Australian population.

This might be why South African sites between 60,000 and 30,000 years old so rarely seem to bear the modern signature: demographic reconstructions suggest that the human population in Africa crashed around 60,000 years ago because of a precipitous drop in temperature. Inferring capacity from what people produced is inherently problematic, White observes. Medieval folks doubtless had the brainpower to go to the moon, he notes. Just because they did not does not mean they were not our cognitive equals. "At any given moment," White reflects, "people don't fulfill their entire potential."

Symbol-Minded

The debate over when, where and how our ancestors became cognitively modern is complicated by the fact that experts disagree over what constitutes modern human behavior in the first place. In the strictest sense, the term encompasses every facet of culture evident today—from agriculture to the iPod. To winnow the definition into something more useful to archaeologists, many workers employ the list of behavioral traits that distinguish the Middle and Upper Paleolithic in Europe. Others use the material cultures of modern and recent hunter-gatherers as a guide. Ultimately, whether or not a set of remains is deemed evidence of modernity can hinge on the preferred definition of the evaluator.

Taking that into consideration, some experts instead advocate focusing on the origin and evolution of arguably the most important characteristic of modern human societies: symbolically organized behavior, including language. "The ability to store symbols externally, outside of the human brain, is the key to everything we do today," Henshilwood asserts. A symbol-based system of communication might not be a perfect proxy for behavioral modernity in the archaeological record, as the Tasmanian example illustrates, but at least researchers seem to accept it as a defining aspect of the human mind as we know it, if not *the* defining aspect.

It remains to be seen just how far back in time symbolic culture arose. And discoveries outside of Africa and Europe are helping to flesh out the story. Controversial evidence from the rock shelters of Malakunanja II and Nauwal-abila I in Australia's Northern Territory, for instance, suggests that people had arrived there by 60,000 years ago. To reach the island continent, emigrants traveling from southeastern Asia would have had to have built

> *Other finds raise the question of whether symbolism is unique to anatomically modern humans.*

sturdy watercraft and navigated a minimum of 50 miles of open water, depending on the sea level. Scholars mostly agree that any human capable of managing this feat must have been fully modern. And in Israel's Qafzeh Cave, Erella Hovers of the Hebrew University of Jerusalem and her team have recovered dozens of pieces of red ochre near 92,000-year-old graves of *H. sapiens*. They believe the lumps of pigment were heated in hearths to achieve a specific hue of scarlet and then used in funerary rituals.

Other finds raise the question of whether symbolism is unique to anatomically modern humans. Neandertal sites commonly contain evidence of systematic ochre processing, and toward the end of their reign in Europe, in the early Upper Paleolithic, Neandertals apparently developed their own cultural tradition of manufacturing body ornaments, as evidenced by the discovery of pierced teeth and other objects at sites such as Quinçay and the Grotte du Renne at Arcy-sur-Cure in France. They also interred their dead. The symbolic nature of this behavior in their case is debated because the burials lack grave goods. But in April 2005, at the annual meeting of the Paleoanthropology Society, Jill Cook of the British Museum reported that digital microscopy of remains from Krapina Rock Shelter in Croatia bolsters the hypothesis that Neandertals were cleaning the bones of the deceased, possibly in a kind of mortuary ritual, as opposed to defleshing them for food.

Perhaps the ability to think symbolically evolved independently in Neandertals and anatomically modern *H. sapiens*. Or maybe it arose before the two groups set off on separate evolutionary trajectories, in a primeval common ancestor. "I can't prove it, but I bet [*Homo*] *heidelbergensis* [a hominid that lived as much as 400,000 years ago] was capable of this," White speculates.

For his part, Henshilwood is betting that the dawn of symbol-driven thinking lies in the Middle Stone Age. After nine field seasons at Blombos, he and his team had sifted through a third of the cave's 75,000-year-old deposits, leaving the rest to future archaeologists with as yet unforeseen advances in excavation and dating techniques. "We don't really need to go further in these levels at Blombos," Henshilwood says. "We need to find other sites now that date to this time period." He is confident that they will succeed in that endeavor, having already identified a number of very promising locales in the coastal De Hoop Nature Reserve, about 30 miles west of Blombos.

Sitting in the courtyard of the African Heritage Research Institute pondering the dainty snail shells in my hand, I consider what they might have represented to the Blombos people. In some ways, it is difficult to imagine our ancient ancestors setting aside basic concerns of food, water, predators and shelter to make such baubles. But later, perusing a Cape Town jeweler's offerings—from cross pendants cast in gold to diamond engagement rings—it is harder still to conceive of *Homo sapiens* behaving any other way. The trinkets may have changed somewhat since 75,000 years ago, but the all-important messages they encode are probably still the same.

More to Explore

The Revolution That Wasn't: A New Interpretation of the Origin of Modern Human Behavior. Sally McBrearty and Alison S. Brooks in *Journal of Human Evolution*, Vol. 39, No. 5, pages 453–563; November 2000.

Emergence of Modern Human Behavior: Middle Stone Age Engravings from South Africa. Christopher S. Henshilwood et al. in *Science*, Vol. 295, pages 1278–1280; February 15, 2002.

The Dawn of Human Culture. Richard G. Klein, with Blake Edgar. John Wiley & Sons, 2002.

The Invisible Frontier: A Multiple Species Model for the Origin of Behavioral Modernity. Francesco d'Errico in *Evolutionary Anthropology*, Vol. 12, No. 4, pages 188–202; August 5, 2003.

The Origin of Modern Human Behavior: Critique of the Models and Their Test Implications. Christopher S. Henshilwood and Curtis W. Marean in *Current Anthropology*, Vol. 44, No. 5, pages 627–651; December 2003.

Prehistoric Art: The Symbolic Journey of Humankind. Randall White, Harry N. Abrams, 2003.

Nassarius kraussianus Shell Beads from Blombos Cave: Evidence for Symbolic Behavior in the Middle Stone Age. Francesco d'Errico, Christopher Henshilwood, Marian Vanhaeren and Karen van Niekerk in *Journal of Human Evolution*, Vol. 48, No. 1, pages 3–24; January 2005.

Early Chefs Left Indelible Mark on Human Evolution

By James Randerson
New Scientist, March 22, 2003

The idea that the invention of cooking fundamentally influenced our evolutionary past has been given a boost by a study of modern diets.

A team of anthropologists conclude that this new found culinary talent is the only way to explain the huge change in our evolution 1.9 million years ago, when Homo erectus appeared.

H. erectus was 60 per cent larger than its predecessors, and sported the largest increase in human brain size ever seen. Some experts believe this growth spurt was fuelled by protein derived from eating raw meat. But Richard Wrangham and NancyLou Conklin-Brittain of Harvard University and Greg Laden of the University of Minnesota say it was triggered by cooking plant food such as roots and tubers.

The heat of cooking smashes open cells and breaks down indigestible fibre into energy-giving carbohydrates. The advent of cooking would therefore account for H. erectus having a smaller gut and teeth, and explain why early humans became more sociable as they brought food back to a central cooking area, the anthropologists say. "We're talking about the beginning of humanity," says Laden.

Wrangham and Conklin-Brittain have new evidence to back this idea. They have found that people need to eat twice as much raw food as cooked food to gain the same energy from a vegetarian diet, and 50 per cent more if it is a diet of meat and plants.

From a study of people in Germany who ate a raw food diet, Wrangham and Conklin-Brittain have calculated that a person eating uncooked, vegetarian food would have to consume around 9 per cent of their body weight each day to get enough calories to maintain a leisurely modern Western lifestyle. That's more food than the average American eats on Thanksgiving Day, they will report in the journal Comparative Biochemistry and Physiology, A.

Adding raw meat to the diet doesn't help much, because uncooked meat takes a long time to chew. Chimpanzees, for example, take hours to finish a monkey carcass and often abandon it after polishing off easy bits such as the brain and liver.

The nutritional limitations of an uncooked diet are obvious even without these calculations. About a third of the raw food eaters in the study in Germany suffered from chronic energy deficiency, and half of the women did not have a regular menstrual cycle. "Cooking enormously improves the quality of food," says Wrangham.

But Henry Bunn, an anthropologist at the University of Winsconsin-Madison, is not convinced. He says there are other ways to make food more nutritious: H. erectus could, for example, have "pre-digested" raw meat and plants by smashing them with stone tools, which is a much simpler adaptation than cooking. Other critics say that there is little evidence that early humans used fire before 300,000 years ago.

But Laden and Wrangham say that physical evidence from fires would be unlikely to have survived millions of years. Whenever cooking did begin though, it would have left an indelible mark on human evolution, they say. The only other such change is the reduction in size in our ancestors' teeth 100,000 years ago.

But this happened hundreds of thousands of years after the advent of fire so is unlikely to have been the result of starting to eat cooked food. If cooking did not influence human evolution at the time of H. erectus, asks Wrangham, then when?

Caveman Crooners May Have Aided Early Human Life

By Sharon Begley
Associated Press Financial Wire, March 31, 2006

In Steven Mithen's imagination, the small band of Neanderthals gathered 50,000 years ago around the caves of Le Moustier, in what is now the Dordogne region of France, were butchering carcasses, scraping skins, shaping ax heads and singing.

One of the fur-clad men started it, a rhythmic sound with rising and falling pitch, and others picked it up, indicating their willingness to cooperate both in the moment and in the future, when the group would have to hunt or fend off predators. The music promoted "a sense of we-ness, of being together in the same situation facing the same problems," suggests Prof. Mithen, an archaeologist at England's Reading University. Music, he says, creates "a social rather than a merely individual identity." And that may solve a longstanding mystery.

Music gives biologists fits. Its ubiquity in human cultures, and strong evidence that the brain comes preloaded with musical circuits, suggest that music is as much a product of human evolution as, say, thumbs. But that raises the question of what music is for. Back in 1871, Darwin speculated that human music, like bird songs, attracts mates. Or, as he put it, prelinguistic human ancestors tried "to charm each other with musical notes and rhythm."

Some scientists today share that view. "Music was shaped by sexual selection to function mostly as a courtship display," Geoffrey Miller, of the University of New Mexico, argued in a 2001 paper. But like Darwin, he bases that conclusion on the belief that music has "no identifiable survival benefits." If a trait doesn't help creatures survive, then it can persist generation after generation only if it helps them reproduce.

Studies in neuroscience and anthropology, however, suggest that music did help human ancestors survive, particularly before language. In "The Singing Neanderthals," which Harvard University Press is publishing Friday, Prof. Mithen weaves those studies into an intriguing argument that "language may have been built on the neural underpinnings of music."

He starts with evidence that music is not merely a side effect of intelligence and language, as some argue. Instead, recent discoveries suggest that music lays sole claim to specific neural real estate. Consider musical savants. Although learning-disabled or retarded, they have astounding musical abilities. One savant could hardly speak or understand words, yet he played flawlessly a simple piano melody from memory despite hearing it only once. In an encore, he added left-hand chords and transposed it into a minor key.

"Music," says Prof. Mithen, "can exist within the brain in the absence of language," a sign that the two evolved independently. And since language impairment does not wipe out musical ability, the latter "must have a longer evolutionary history."

With music in the brain, early humans had the neural foundation for the development of what most distinguishes us from other animals: symbolic thought and language.

In the opposite of musical savantism, people with "amusia" can't perceive changes in rhythm, identify melodies they've heard before or recognize changes in pitch. Since they have normal hearing and language, the problem must lie in brain circuits that are music-specific.

More evidence that the brain has dedicated, inborn musical circuits is that even babies have musical preferences, finds Sandra Trehub of the University of Toronto. They listen longer to perfect fifths and perfect fourths, and look pained by minor thirds.

If music is indeed an innate, stand-alone adaptation, then evolution could have nursed it along over the eons only if it helped early humans survive. It did so, Prof. Mithen suggests, because "if music is about anything, it is about expressing and inducing emotion."

Particular notes elicit the same emotions from most people, regardless of culture, studies suggest. A major third (prominent in Beethoven's "Ode to Joy") sounds happy; a minor third (as in the gloomy first movements of Mahler's Fifth) provokes feelings of sadness and even doom. A major seventh expresses aspiration. The absence of a third seems unresolved, loose, as if hanging, adds jazz guitarist Michael Rood, 17 years old.

The fact that listeners hear the same emotion in a given musical score is something a Neanderthal crooner might have exploited. Music can manipulate people's emotional states (think of liturgical music, martial music or workplace music). Happy people are more cooperative and creative. By fostering cooperation and creativity among bands of early, prelanguage human ancestors, music would have given them a survival edge. "If you can manipulate other people's emotions," says Prof. Mithen, "you have an advantage."

Music also promotes social bonding, which was crucial when humans were more often hunted than hunter and finding food was no walk on the savannah. Proto-music "became a communication system" for "the expression of emotion and the forging of group identities," argues Prof. Mithen.

Because music has grammar-like qualities such as recursion, it might have served an even greater function. With music in the brain, early humans had the neural foundation for the development of what most distinguishes us from other animals: symbolic thought and language.

Appendix

Was the World Made for Man?

By Mark Twain, 1903

"Alfred Russell Wallace's revival of the theory that this earth is at the centre of the stellar universe, and is the only habitable globe, has aroused great interest in the world."—*Literary Digest*

"For ourselves we do thoroughly believe that man, as he lives just here on this tiny earth, is in essence and possibilities the most sublime existence in all the range of non-divine being—the chief love and delight of God."—Chicago "Interior" (Presb.)

I seem to be the only scientist and theologian still remaining to be heard from on this important matter of whether the world was made for man or not. I feel that it is time for me to speak.

I stand almost with the others. They believe the world was made for man, I believe it likely that it was made for man; they think there is proof, astronomical mainly, that it was made for man, I think there is evidence only, not proof, that it was made for him. It is too early, yet, to arrange the verdict, the returns are not all in. When they are all in, I think they will show that the world was made for man; but we must not hurry, we must patiently wait till they are all in.

Now as far as we have got, astronomy is on our side. Mr. Wallace has clearly shown this. He has clearly shown two things: that the world was made for man, and that the universe was made for the world—to stiddy it, you know. The astronomy part is settled, and cannot be challenged.

We come now to the geological part. This is the one where the evidence is not all in, yet. It is coming in, hourly, daily, coming in all the time, but naturally it comes with geological carefulness and deliberation, and we must not be impatient, we must not get excited, we must be calm, and wait. To lose our tranquillity will not hurry geology; nothing hurries geology.

It takes a long time to prepare a world for man, such a thing is not done in a day. Some of the great scientists, carefully ciphering the evidences furnished by geology, have arrived at the conviction that our world is prodigiously old, and they may be right, but Lord Kelvin is not of their opinion. He takes a cautious, conservative view, in order to be on the safe side, and feels sure it is not so old as they think. As Lord Kelvin is the highest authority in science now living, I think we must yield to him and accept his view. He does not concede that the world is more than a hundred million years old. He believes it is that old, but not older. Lyell believed that our race was introduced into the world 31,000 years ago, Herbert Spencer makes it 32,000. Lord Kelvin agrees with Spencer.

Very well. According to Kelvin's figures it took 99,968,000 years to prepare the world for man, impatient as the Creator doubtless was to see him and admire him. But a large enterprise like this has to be conducted warily, painstakingly, logically. It was foreseen that man would have to have the oyster. Therefore the first preparation was made for the oyster. Very well, you cannot make an oyster out of whole cloth, you must make the oyster's ancestor first. This is not done in a day. You must make a vast variety of invertebrates, to start with—belemnites, trilobites, jebusites, amalekites, and that sort of fry, and put them to soak in a primary sea, and wait and see what will happen. Some will be a disappointment—the belemnites, the ammonites and such; they will be failures, they will die out and become extinct, in the course of the 19,000,000 years covered by the experiment, but all is not lost, for the amalekites will fetch the home-stake; they will develop gradually into encrinites, and stalactites, and blatherskites, and one thing and another as the mighty ages creep on and the Archaean and the Cambrian Periods pile their lofty crags in the primordial seas, and at last the first grand stage in the preparation of the world for man stands completed, the Oyster is done. An oyster has hardly any more reasoning power than a scientist has; and so it is reasonably certain that this one jumped to the conclusion that the nineteen-million years was a preparation for *him*; but that would be just like an oyster, which is the most conceited animal there is, except man. And anyway, this one could not know, at that early date, that he was only an incident in a scheme, and that there was some more to the scheme, yet.

The oyster being achieved, the next thing to be arranged for in the preparation of the world for man, was fish. Fish, and coal to fry it with. So the Old Silurian seas were opened up to breed the fish in, and at the same time the great work of building Old Red Sandstone mountains 80,000 feet high to cold-storage their fossils in was begun. This latter was quite indispensable, for there would be no end of failures again, no end of extinctions—millions of them—and it would be cheaper and less trouble to can them in the rocks than keep tally of them in a book. One does not build the coal beds and 80,000 feet of perpendicular Old Red Sandstone in a brief time—no, it took twenty million years. In the first place, a coal bed is a slow and troublesome and tiresome thing to construct. You have to grow prodigious forests of tree-ferns and reeds and calamites and such things in a marshy region; then you have to sink them under out of sight and let them rot; then you have to turn the streams on them, so as to bury them under several feet of sediment, and the sediment must have time to harden and turn to rock; next you must grow another forest on top, then sink it and put on another layer of sediment and harden it; then more forest and more rock, layer upon layer, three miles deep—ah, indeed it is a sickening slow job to build a coal-measure and do it right!

So the millions of years drag on; and meantime the fish-culture is lazying along and frazzling out in a way to make a person tired. You have developed ten thousand kinds of fishes from the oyster; and come to look, you have raised nothing but fossils, nothing but extinctions. There is nothing left alive and progressive but a ganoid or two and perhaps half a dozen asteroids. Even the cat wouldn't eat such.

Still, it is no great matter; there is plenty of time, yet, and they will develop into something tasty before man is ready for them. Even a ganoid can be depended on for that, when he is not going to be called on for sixty million years.

The Palaeozoic time-limit having now been reached, it was necessary to begin the next stage in the preparation of the world for man, by opening up the Mesozoic Age and instituting some reptiles. For man would need reptiles. Not to eat, but to develop himself from. This being the most important detail of the scheme, a spacious liberality of time was set apart for it—thirty million years. What wonders followed! From the remaining ganoids and asteroids and alkaloids were developed by slow and steady and pains-taking culture those stupendous saurians that used to prowl about the steamy world in those remote ages, with their snaky heads reared forty feet in the air and sixty feet of body and tail racing and thrashing after. All gone, now, alas—all extinct, except the little handful of Arkansawrians left stranded and lonely with us here upon this far-flung verge and fringe of time.

Yes, it took thirty million years and twenty million reptiles to get one that would stick long enough to develop into something else and let the scheme proceed to the next step.

Then the Pterodactyl burst upon the world in all his impressive solemnity and grandeur, and all Nature recognized that the Cainozoic threshold was crossed and a new Period open for business, a new stage begun in the preparation of the globe for man. It may be that the Pterodactyl thought the thirty million years had been intended as a preparation for himself, for there was nothing too foolish for a Pterodactyl to imagine, but he was in error, the preparation was for man, Without doubt the Pterodactyl attracted great attention, for even the least observant could see that there was the making of a bird in him. And so it turned out. Also the makings of a mammal, in time. One thing we have to say to his credit, that in the matter of picturesqueness he was the triumph of his Period; he wore wings and had teeth, and was a starchy and wonderful mixture altogether, a kind of long-distance premonitory symptom of Kipling's marine:

> 'E isn't one o' the reg'lar Line, nor 'e isn't one of the crew,
> 'E's a kind of a giddy harumfrodite [hermaphrodite]—soldier an' sailor too!

From this time onward for nearly another thirty million years the preparation moved briskly. From the Pterodactyl was developed the bird; from the bird the kangaroo, from the kangaroo the other marsupials; from these the mastodon, the megatherium, the giant sloth, the Irish elk, and all that crowd that you make useful and instructive fossils out of—then came the first great Ice Sheet, and they all retreated before it and crossed over the bridge at Behring's strait and wandered around over Europe and Asia and died. All except a few, to carry on the preparation with. Six Glacial Periods with two million years between Periods chased these poor orphans up and down and about the earth, from weather to weather—from tropic swelter at the poles to Arctic frost at the equator and back again and to and fro, they never knowing what kind of weather was going to turn up next; and if ever they settled down anywhere the whole continent suddenly sank under them without the least notice and they had to trade places with the fishes and scramble off to where the seas had been, and scarcely a dry rag on them; and when there was nothing else doing a volcano would let go and fire them out from wherever they had located. They led this unsettled and irritating life for twenty-five million years, half the time afloat, half the time aground, and always wondering what it was all for, they never suspecting, of course, that it was a preparation for man and had to be done just so or it wouldn't be any proper and harmonious place for him when he arrived.

And at last came the monkey, and anybody could see that man wasn't far off, now. And in truth that was so. The monkey went on developing for close upon 5,000,000 years, and then turned into a man—to all appearances.

Such is the history of it. Man has been here 32,000 years. That it took a hundred million years to prepare the world for him is proof that that is what it was done for. I suppose it is. I dunno. If the Eiffel tower were now representing the world's age, the skin of paint on the pinnacle-knob at its summit would represent man's share of that age; and anybody would perceive that that skin was what the tower was built for. I reckon they would, I dunno.

Kitzmiller, et al. v. Dover Area School District, et al.

UNITED STATES DISTRICT COURT FOR THE MIDDLE DISTRICT OF PENNSYLVANIA CASE
  NO. 04CV2688
JUDGE JONES

Memorandum Opinion, December 20, 2005

Introduction

On October 18, 2004, the Defendant Dover Area School Board of Directors passed by a 6–3 vote the following resolution: Students will be made aware of gaps/problems in Darwin's theory and of other theories of evolution including, but not limited to, intelligent design. Note: Origins of Life is not taught.

On November 19, 2004, the Defendant Dover Area School District announced by press release that, commencing in January 2005, teachers would be required to read the following statement to students in the ninth grade biology class at Dover High School:

The Pennsylvania Academic Standards require students to learn about Darwin's Theory of Evolution and eventually to take a standardized test of which evolution is a part.

Because Darwin's Theory is a theory, it continues to be tested as new evidence is discovered. The Theory is not a fact. Gaps in the Theory exist for which there is no evidence. A theory is defined as a well-tested explanation that unifies a broad range of observations.

Intelligent Design is an explanation of the origin of life that differs from Darwin's view. The reference book, Of Pandas and People, is available for students who might be interested in gaining an understanding of what Intelligent Design actually involves.

With respect to any theory, students are encouraged to keep an open mind. The school leaves the discussion of the Origins of Life to individual students and their families. As a Standards-driven district, class instruction focuses upon preparing students to achieve proficiency on Standards-based assessments.

H. Conclusion

The proper application of both the endorsement and Lemon tests to the facts of this case makes it abundantly clear that the Board's ID Policy violates the Establishment Clause. In making this determination, we have addressed the

---

Web site of the U.S. District Court for the Middle District of Pennsylvania, *www.pamd.uscourts.gov*

seminal question of whether ID is science. We have concluded that it is not, and moreover that ID cannot uncouple itself from its creationist, and thus religious, antecedents.

Both Defendants and many of the leading proponents of ID make a bedrock assumption which is utterly false. Their presupposition is that evolutionary theory is antithetical to a belief in the existence of a supreme being and to religion in general. Repeatedly in this trial, Plaintiffs' scientific experts testified that the theory of evolution represents good science, is overwhelmingly accepted by the scientific community, and that it in no way conflicts with, nor does it deny, the existence of a divine creator.

To be sure, Darwin's theory of evolution is imperfect. However, the fact that a scientific theory cannot yet render an explanation on every point should not be used as a pretext to thrust an untestable alternative hypothesis grounded in religion into the science classroom or to misrepresent well-established scientific propositions.

The citizens of the Dover area were poorly served by the members of the Board who voted for the ID Policy. It is ironic that several of these individuals, who so staunchly and proudly touted their religious convictions in public, would time and again lie to cover their tracks and disguise the real purpose behind the ID Policy.

With that said, we do not question that many of the leading advocates of ID have *bona fide* and deeply held beliefs which drive their scholarly endeavors. Nor do we controvert that ID should continue to be studied, debated, and discussed. As stated, our conclusion today is that it is unconstitutional to teach ID as an alternative to evolution in a public school science classroom.

Those who disagree with our holding will likely mark it as the product of an activist judge. If so, they will have erred as this is manifestly not an activist Court. Rather, this case came to us as the result of the activism of an ill-informed faction on a school board, aided by a national public interest law firm eager to find a constitutional test case on ID, who in combination drove the Board to adopt an imprudent and ultimately unconstitutional policy. The breathtaking inanity of the Board's decision is evident when considered against the factual backdrop which has now been fully revealed through this trial. The students, parents, and teachers of the Dover Area School District deserved better than to be dragged into this legal maelstrom, with its resulting utter waste of monetary and personal resources.

To preserve the separation of church and state mandated by the Establishment Clause of the First Amendment to the United States Constitution, and Art. I, § 3 of the Pennsylvania Constitution, we will enter an order permanently enjoining Defendants from maintaining the ID Policy in any school within the Dover Area School District, from requiring teachers to denigrate or disparage the scientific theory of evolution, and from requiring teachers to refer to a religious, alternative theory known as ID. We will also issue a declaratory judgment that Plaintiffs' rights under the Constitutions of the United States and the Commonwealth of Pennsylvania have been violated by Defendants' actions. Defendants' actions in violation of Plaintiffs' civil rights as guaranteed to them by the Constitution of the United States and 42 U.S.C. § 1983 subject Defendants to liability with respect to injunctive and declaratory relief, but also for nominal damages and the reasonable value of Plaintiffs' attorneys' services and costs incurred in vindicating Plaintiffs' constitutional rights.

Edwards, Governor of Louisiana, et al. v. Aguillard et al.

SUPREME COURT OF THE UNITED STATES
482 U.S. 578

December 10, 1986, Argued

June 19, 1987, Decided

Justice Brennan delivered the opinion of the Court.

I

The Creationism Act forbids the teaching of the theory of evolution in public schools unless accompanied by instruction in "creation science." No school is required to teach evolution or creation science. If either is taught, however, the other must also be taught. Ibid. The theories of evolution and creation science are statutorily defined as "the scientific evidences for [creation or evolution] and inferences from those scientific evidences."

Appellees, who include parents of children attending Louisiana public schools, Louisiana teachers, and religious leaders, challenged the constitutionality of the Act in District Court, seeking an injunction and declaratory relief. Appellants, Louisiana officials charged with implementing the Act, defended on the ground that the purpose of the Act is to protect a legitimate secular interest, namely, academic freedom. Appellees attacked the Act as facially invalid because it violated the Establishment Clause and made a motion for summary judgment. The District Court granted the motion. The court held that there can be no valid secular reason for prohibiting the teaching of evolution, a theory historically opposed by some religious denominations. The court further concluded that "the teaching of 'creation-science' and 'creationism,' as contemplated by the statute, involves teaching 'tailored to the principles' of a particular religious sect or group of sects." The District Court therefore held that the Creationism Act violated the Establishment Clause either because it prohibited the teaching of evolution or because it required the teaching of creation science with the purpose of advancing a particular religious doctrine. The court of Appeals affirmed. We noted probable jurisdiction, and now affirm.

II

The Establishment Clause forbids the enactment of any law "respecting an establishment of religion." The Court has applied a three-pronged test to determine whether legislation comports with the Establishment Clause. First, the legislature must have adopted the law with a secular purpose. Second, the statute's principal or primary effect must be one that neither advances nor inhibits religion. Third, the statute must not result in an excessive entanglement of government with religion. Lemon v. Kurtzman (1971). State action violates the Establishment Clause if it fails to satisfy any of these prongs.

In this case, the Court must determine whether the Establishment Clause was violated in the special context of the public elementary and secondary school system. States and local school boards are generally afforded considerable discretion in operating public schools. "At the same time . . . we have necessarily recognized that the discretion of the States and local school boards in matters of education must be exercised in a manner that comports with the transcendent imperatives of the First Amendment. . . ."

Therefore, in employing the three-pronged Lemon test, we must do so mindful of the particular concerns that arise in the context of public elementary and secondary schools. We now turn to the evaluation of the Act under the Lemon test.

III

Lemon's first prong focuses on the purpose that animated adoption of the Act. "The purpose prong of the Lemon test asks whether government's actual purpose is to endorse or disapprove of religion." A governmental intention to promote religion is clear when the State enacts a law to serve a religious purpose. This intention may be evidenced by promotion of religion in general or by advancement of a particular religious belief. If the law was enacted for the purpose of endorsing religion, "no consideration of the second or third criteria [of Lemon] is necessary." In this case, appellants have identified no clear secular purpose for the Louisiana Act.

True, the Act's stated purpose is to protect academic freedom. This phrase might, in common parlance, be understood as referring to enhancing the freedom of teachers to teach what they will. The Court of Appeals, however, correctly concluded that the Act was not designed to further that goal. We find no merit in the State's argument that the "legislature may not [have] used the terms 'academic freedom' in the correct legal sense. They might have [had] in mind, instead, a basic concept of fairness; teaching all of the evidence." Even if "academic freedom" is read to mean "teaching all of the evidence" with respect to the origin of human beings, the Act does not further this purpose. The goal of providing a more comprehensive science curriculum is not furthered either by outlawing the teaching of evolution or by requiring the teaching of creation science.

While the Court is normally deferential to a State's articulation of a secular purpose, it is required that the statement of such purpose be sincere and not a sham. It is clear from the legislative history that the purpose of the legislative sponsor, Senator Bill Keith, was to narrow the science curriculum. During the legislative hearings, Senator Keith stated: "My preference would be that neither [creationism nor evolution] be taught." Such a ban on teaching does not promote—indeed, it undermines—the provision of a comprehensive scientific education.

It is equally clear that requiring schools to teach creation science with evolution does not advance academic freedom. The Act does not grant teachers a flexibility that they did not already possess to supplant the present science curriculum with the presentation of theories, besides evolution, about the origin of life. Indeed, the Court of Appeals found that no law prohibited Louisiana public school teachers from teaching any scientific theory. As the president of the Louisiana Science Teachers Association testified, "any scientific concept that's based on established fact can be included in our curriculum already, and no legislation allowing this is necessary." The Act provides Louisiana schoolteachers with no new authority. Thus the stated purpose is not furthered by it.

The Alabama statute held unconstitutional in Wallace v. Jaffree, supra, is analogous. In Wallace, the State characterized its new law as one designed to provide a 1-minute period for meditation. We rejected that stated purpose as insufficient, because a previously adopted Alabama law already provided for such a 1-minute period. Thus, in this case, as in Wallace, "appellants have not identified any secular purpose that was not fully served by [existing state law] before the enactment of [the statute in question]."

Furthermore, the goal of basic "fairness" is hardly furthered by the Act's discriminatory preference for the teaching of creation science and against the teaching of evolution. While requiring that curriculum guides be developed for creation science, the Act says nothing of comparable guides for evolution. Similarly, resource services are supplied for creation science but not for evolution. Only "creation scientists" can serve on the panel that supplies the resource services. The Act forbids school boards to discriminate against anyone who "chooses to be a creation-scientist" or to teach "creationism," but fails to protect those who choose to teach evolution or any other noncreation science theory, or who refuse to teach creation science.

If the Louisiana Legislature's purpose was solely to maximize the comprehensiveness and effectiveness of science instruction, it would have encouraged the teaching of all scientific theories about the origins of humankind. But under the Act's requirements, teachers who were once free to teach any and all facets of this subject are now unable to do so. Moreover, the Act fails even to ensure that creation science will be taught, but instead requires the teaching of this theory only when the theory of evolution is taught. Thus we agree with the Court of Appeals' conclusion that the Act does not serve to protect academic freedom, but has the distinctly different purpose of discrediting "evolution by counterbalancing its teaching at every turn with the teaching of creationism . . ."

It was this link that concerned the Court in Epperson v. Arkansas, 393 U.S. 97 (1968), which also involved a facial challenge to a statute regulating the teaching of evolution. In that case, the Court reviewed an Arkansas statute that made it unlawful for an instructor to teach evolution or to use a textbook that referred to this scientific theory. Although the Arkansas antievolution law did not explicitly state its predominate religious purpose, the Court could not ignore that "the statute was a product of the upsurge of 'fundamentalist' religious fervor" that has long viewed this particular scientific theory as contradicting the literal interpretation of the Bible.

These same historic and contemporaneous antagonisms between the teachings of certain religious denominations and the teaching of evolution are present in this case. The preeminent purpose of the Louisiana Legislature was clearly to advance the religious viewpoint that a supernatural being created humankind. The term "creation science" was defined as embracing this particular religious doctrine by those responsible for the passage of the Creationism Act. Senator Keith's leading expert on creation science, Edward Boudreaux, testified at the legislative hearings that the theory of creation science included belief in the existence of a supernatural creator. Senator Keith also cited testimony from other experts to support the creation-science view that "a creator [was] responsible for the universe and everything in it." The legislative history therefore reveals that the term "creation science," as contemplated by the legislature that adopted this Act, embodies the religious belief that a supernatural creator was responsible for the creation of humankind.

Furthermore, it is not happenstance that the legislature required the teaching of a theory that coincided with this religious view. The legislative history documents that the Act's primary purpose was to change the science curriculum of public schools in order to provide persuasive advantage to a particular religious doctrine that rejects the factual basis of evolution in its entirety. The sponsor of the Creationism Act, Senator Keith, explained during the legislative hearings that his disdain for the theory of evolution resulted from the support that evolution supplied to views contrary to his own religious beliefs. According to Senator Keith, the theory of evolution was consonant with the "cardinal principle[s] of religious humanism, secular humanism, theological liberalism, aetheistism [sic]."

In this case, the purpose of the Creationism Act was to restructure the science curriculum to conform with a particular religious viewpoint. Out of many possible science subjects taught in the public schools, the legislature chose to affect the teaching of the one scientific theory that historically has been opposed by certain religious sects. As in Epperson, the legislature passed the Act to give preference to those religious groups which have as one of their tenets the creation of humankind by a divine creator. The "overriding fact" that confronted the Court in Epperson was "that Arkansas' law selects from the body of knowledge a particular segment which it proscribes for the sole reason that it is deemed to conflict with . . . a particular interpretation of the Book of Genesis by a particular religious group." Similarly, the Creationism Act is designed either to promote the theory of creation science which embodies a particular religious tenet by requiring that creation science be taught whenever evolution is taught or to prohibit the teaching of a scientific theory disfavored by certain religious sects by forbidding the teaching of evolution when creation science is not also taught. The Establishment Clause, however, "forbids alike the preference of a religious doctrine or the prohibition of theory which is deemed antagonistic to a particular dogma."

The Louisiana Creationism Act advances a religious doctrine by requiring either the banishment of the theory of evolution from public school classrooms or the presentation of a religious viewpoint that rejects evolution in its entirety. The Act violates the Establishment Clause of the First Amendment because it seeks to employ the symbolic and financial support of government to achieve a religious purpose. The judgment of the Court of Appeals therefore is

Affirmed.

Justice Scalia, with whom the Chief Justice joins, dissenting.

Even if I agreed with the questionable premise that legislation can be invalidated under the Establishment Clause on the basis of its motivation alone, without regard to its effects, I would still find no justification for today's decision. The Louisiana legislators who passed the "Balanced Treatment for Creation-Science and Evolution-Science Act", each of whom had sworn to support the Constitution, were well aware of the potential Establishment Clause problems and considered that aspect of the legislation with great care. After seven hearings and several months of study, resulting in substantial revision of the original proposal, they approved the Act overwhelmingly and specifically articulated the secular purpose they meant it to serve. Although the record contains abundant evidence of the sincerity of that purpose (the only issue pertinent to this case), the Court today holds, essentially on the basis of "its visceral knowledge regarding what must have motivated the legislators," that the members of the Louisiana Legislature knowingly violated their oaths and then lied about it. I dissent. Had requirements of the Balanced Treatment Act that are not apparent on its face been clarified by an interpretation of the Louisiana Supreme Court, or by the manner of its implementation, the Act might well be found unconstitutional; but the question of its constitutionality cannot rightly be disposed of on the gallop, by impugning the motives of its supporters.

I

This case arrives here in the following posture: The Louisiana Supreme Court has never been given an opportunity to interpret the Balanced Treatment Act, State officials have never attempted to implement it, and it has never been the subject of a full evidentiary hearing. We can only guess at its meaning. We know that it forbids instruction in either "creation-science" or "evolution-science" without instruction in the other, but the parties are sharply divided over what creation science consists of. Appellants insist that it is a collection of educationally valuable scientific data that has been censored from classrooms by an embarrassed scientific establishment. Appellees insist it is not science at all but thinly veiled religious doctrine. Both interpretations of the intended meaning of that phrase find considerable support in the legislative history.

At least at this stage in the litigation, it is plain to me that we must accept appellants' view of what the statute means. To begin with, the statute itself defines "creation-science" as "the scientific evidences for creation and inferences from those scientific evidences." If, however, that definition is not thought sufficiently helpful, the means by which the Louisiana Supreme Court will give the term more precise content is quite clear—and again, at this stage in the litigation, favors the appellants' view. "Creation science" is unquestionably a "term of art," and thus, under Louisiana law, is "to be interpreted according to [its] received meaning and acceptance with the learned in the art, trade or profession to which [it] refer[s]." The only evidence in the record of the "received meaning and acceptance" of "creation science" is found in five affidavits filed by appellants. In those affidavits, two scientists, a philosopher, a theologian, and an educator, all of whom claim extensive knowledge of creation science, swear that it is essentially a collection of scientific data supporting the theory that the physical universe and life within it appeared suddenly and have not changed substantially since appearing. These experts insist that creation science is a strictly scientific concept that can be presented without religious reference. At this point, then, we must assume that the Balanced Treatment Act does not require the presentation of religious doctrine. . . .

A few principles have emerged from our cases, principles which should, but to an unfortunately large extent do not, guide the Court's application of *Lemon* today. It is clear, first of all, that regardless of what "legislative purpose" may mean in other contexts, for the purpose of the Lemon test it means the "actual" motives of those responsible for the challenged action. Thus, if those legislators who supported the Balanced Treatment Act in fact acted with a "sincere" secular purpose, the Act survives the first component of the Lemon test, regardless of whether that purpose is likely to be achieved by the provisions they enacted.

Our cases have also confirmed that when the Lemon Court referred to "a secular . . . purpose," it meant "a secular purpose." The author of Lemon, writing for the Court, has said that invalidation under the purpose prong is appropriate when "there [is] no question that the statute or activity was motivated wholly by religious considerations." Thus, the majority's invalidation of the Balanced Treatment Act is defensible only if the record indicates that the Louisiana Legislature had no secular purpose.

It is important to stress that the purpose forbidden by Lemon is the purpose to "advance religion." Our cases in no way imply that the Establishment Clause forbids legislators merely to act upon their religious convictions. We surely would not strike down a law providing money to feed the hungry or shelter the homeless if it could be demonstrated that, but for the religious beliefs of the legislators, the funds would not have been approved. Also, political activism by the religiously motivated is part of our heritage. Notwithstanding the majority's implication to the contrary we do not presume that the sole purpose of a law is to advance religion merely because it was supported strongly by organized religions or by adherents of particular faiths. To do so would deprive religious men and women of their right to participate in the political process. Today's religious activism may give us the Balanced Treatment Act, but yesterday's resulted in the abolition of slavery, and tomorrow's may bring relief for famine victims.

Similarly, we will not presume that a law's purpose is to advance religion merely because it "'happens to coincide or harmonize with the tenets of some or all religions,'" or because it benefits religion, even substantially. We have, for example, turned back Establishment Clause challenges to restrictions on abortion funding, and to Sunday closing laws despite the fact that both "agre[e] with the dictates of [some] Judaeo-Christian religions." Thus, the fact that creation science coincides with the beliefs of certain religions, a fact upon which the majority relies heavily, does not itself justify invalidation of the Act.

Finally, our cases indicate that even certain kinds of governmental actions undertaken with the specific intention of improving the position of religion do not "advance religion" as that term is used in Lemon. Rather, we have said that in at least two circumstances government must act to advance religion, and that in a third it may do so.

With the foregoing in mind, I now turn to the purposes underlying adoption of the Balanced Treatment Act.

II

At the outset, it is important to note that the Balanced Treatment Act did not fly through the Louisiana Legislature on wings of fundamentalist religious fervor—which would be unlikely, in any event, since only a small minority of the State's citizens belong to fundamentalist religious denominations. The Act had its genesis (so to speak) in legislation introduced by Senator Bill Keith in June 1980.

Before summarizing the testimony of Senator Keith and his supporters, I wish to make clear that I by no means intend to endorse its accuracy. But my views (and the views of this Court) about creation science and evolution are (or should be) beside the point. Our task is not to judge the debate about teaching the origins of life, but to ascertain what the members of the Louisiana Legislature believed. The vast majority of them voted to approve a bill which explicitly stated a secular purpose; what is crucial is not their wisdom in believing that purpose would be achieved by the bill, but their sincerity in believing it would be.

Most of the testimony in support of Senator Keith's bill came from the Senator himself and from scientists and educators he presented, many of whom enjoyed academic credentials that may have been regarded as quite impressive by members of the Louisiana Legislature. To a substantial extent, their testimony was devoted to lengthy, and, to the layman, seemingly expert scientific expositions on the origin of life. These scientific lectures touched upon, inter alia, biology, paleontology, genetics, astronomy, astrophysics, probability analysis, and biochemistry. The witnesses repeatedly assured committee members that "hundreds and hundreds" of highly respected, internationally renowned scientists believed in creation science and would support their testimony.

Senator Keith repeatedly and vehemently denied that his purpose was to advance a particular religious doctrine. At the outset of the first hearing on the legislation, he testified: "We are not going to say today that you should have some kind of religious instructions in our schools. . . . We are not talking about religion today. . . . I am not proposing that we take the Bible in each science class and read the first chapter of Genesis."

We have no way of knowing, of course, how many legislators believed the testimony of Senator Keith and his witnesses. But in the absence of evidence to the contrary, we have to assume that many of them did. Given that assumption, the Court today plainly errs in holding that the Louisiana Legislature passed the Balanced Treatment Act for exclusively religious purposes.

Even with nothing more than this legislative history to go on, I think it would be extraordinary to invalidate the Balanced Treatment Act for lack of a valid secular purpose. Striking down a law approved by the democratically elected representatives of the people is no minor matter. "The cardinal principle of statutory construction is to save and not to destroy. We have repeatedly held that as between two possible interpretations of a statute, by one of which it would be unconstitutional and by the other valid, our plain duty is to adopt that which will save the act. . . ."

Because I believe that the Balanced Treatment Act had a secular purpose, which is all the first component of the Lemon test requires, I would reverse the judgment of the Court of Appeals and remand for further consideration.

Bibliography

Books

Darwin, Charles. *On the Origin of Species by Means of Natural Selection*. London: J. Murray, 1859.

Dawkins, Richard. *The Ancestor's Tale: A Pilgrimage to the Dawn of Evolution*. New York: Houghton Mifflin, 2004.

———. *Climbing Mount Improbable*. New York: W. W. Norton & Company, 1997.

———. *River out of Eden: A Darwinian View of Life*. New York: HarperCollins, 1996.

———. *The Selfish Gene: 30th Anniversary Edition*. New York: Oxford University Press, 2006.

Diamond, Jared. *The Third Chimpanzee: The Evolution and Future of the Human Animal*. New York: Harper Perennial, 1992.

———. *Why Is Sex Fun?: The Evolution of Human Sexuality*. New York: Basic Books, 1998.

Ehrlich, Paul R. *Human Natures: Genes, Cultures, and the Human Prospect*. New York: Penguin, 2002.

Gould, Stephen Jay. *The Book of Life: An Illustrated History of the Evolution of Life on Earth*. New York: W. W. Norton, 2001.

———. *Ever Since Darwin: Reflections on Natural History*. New York: W. W. Norton, 1999.

———. *Hen's Teeth and Horse's Toes*. New York: W. W. Norton, 1994.

———. *Rocks of Ages: Science and Religion in the Fullness of Life*. New York: Ballantine Books, 1999.

———. *The Structure of Evolutionary Theory*. Cambridge, Mass.: Belknap Press, 2002.

Hrdy, Sarah Blaffer. *Mother Nature: Maternal Instincts and How They Shape the Human Species*. New York: Ballantine Books, 2000.

———. *The Woman That Never Evolved*. Cambridge, Mass.: Harvard University Press, 2005.

Larson, Edward J. *Evolution: The Remarkable History of a Scientific Theory*. New York: Modern Library, 2004.

———. *Summer for the Gods: The Scopes Trial and America's Continuing Debate over Science and Religion*. Cambridge, Mass.: Harvard University Press, 2005.

———. *Trial and Error: The American Controversy Over Creation and Evolution*. New York: Oxford University Press, 2003.

Mayr, Ernst. *One Long Argument: Charles Darwin and the Genesis of Modern Evolutionary Thought*. Cambridge, Mass.: Harvard University Press, 2005.

———. *What Evolution Is*. New York: Basic Books, 2001.

The National Academy of Sciences. *Science and Creationism: A View from the National Academy of Sciences.* Washington, D.C.: National Academies Press, 1999.

Ridley, Mark. *Evolution.* Malden, Mass.: Blackwell Science, 2004.

Ridley, Matt. *Genome: The Autobiography of a Species in 23 Chapters.* New York: HarperCollins, 1999.

———. *Nature Via Nurture: Genes, Experience, and What Makes Us Human.* New York: HarperCollins, 1999.

———. *The Red Queen: Sex and the Evolution of Human Nature.* New York: Harper Perennial, 2003.

Scott, Eugenie. *Evolution vs. Creationism: An Introduction.* Los Angeles: University of California Press, 2004.

Wilson, Edward O. *Sociobiology: The New Synthesis.* Cambridge, Mass.: Belknap Press, 2002.

Web Sites

Readers seeking additional information about evolution may wish to refer to the following Web sites, all of which were operational as of this writing.

American Museum of Natural History
http://www.amnh.org/

In addition to highlighting specimens from the museum's extensive zoology and paleontology collections, this Web site includes an extensive section on the life of Charles Darwin and the influence that his ideas have had on the development of the life sciences.

Charles Darwin Foundation
http://www.darwinfoundation.org/

The Charles Darwin Foundation was established in 1959 to conserve the ecosystems in the Galapagos Archipelago—the site that inspired Darwin's theory of evolution—and its surrounding Marine Reserve. The Foundation operates the Charles Darwin Research Station located in the Galapagos Islands, which conducts scientific research and provides environmental education for conservation.

National Museum of Natural History, Smithsonian Institution
http://www.mnh.si.edu/

The museum's Web site includes information on paleobiology, invertebrate zoology, and vertebrate zoology, as well as topical sections on evolution.

Natural History Magazine
http://www.naturalhistorymag.com/

Holding longstanding affiliations with leading science centers and museums, including the American Museum of Natural History, *Natural History* magazine offers readers an in-depth view of nature, science, and culture. It has featured extensive articles on evolution from several disciplinary angles, such as anthropology, paleontology, and biology, among others.

Public Broadcasting Service: Evolution Project
http://www.pbs.org/wgbh/evolution/

The Public Broadcasting Service is a national nonprofit media venture whose aim is to provide commercial-free quality programs and educational resources to the American public. As part of a seven-part television broadcast series, PBS launched the *Evolution* project Web site, along with an educational outreach initiative, to inform viewers about the impact of evolutionary science on society and culture, dispel commonly held misconceptions, and foster dialogue and debate.

Understanding Evolution
http://evolution.berkeley.edu/

Understanding Evolution is a joint noncommercial project of the University of California Museum of Paleontology and the National Center for Science Education. The Web site offers both students and instructors the history of, research on, and latest developments in the field of evolutionary biology.

Additional Periodical Articles with Abstracts

More information about evolution and related subjects can be found in the following articles. Readers who require a more comprehensive selection are advised to consult the *Readers' Guide Abstracts* and other H.W. Wilson publications.

Fade to White. Beth Geiger. *Current Science*, v. 91 pp6–7 January 6, 2006.

White Sands National Monument in New Mexico wasn't always white. It was brown. About 6,000 years ago a shift in geology turned it white. Now, as Geiger explains, the lizards at White Sands have adapted to that change by turning white too.

Dinosaurs. Carl Zimmer. *Discover*, v. 26 pp32–9 April 2005.

Nine questions concerning dinosaurs that continue to perplex paleontologists despite the recent preponderance of new fossil discoveries are discussed. The questions relate to why dinosaurs conquered the planet 210 million years ago and grew so big, whether dinosaurs were warm blooded, how fast Tyrannosaurus rex and other predatory dinosaurs could run, whether dinosaurs were social animals and good parents, the unusual facial features of Triceratops and its relatives, how some dinosaurs evolved feathers and some feathered dinosaurs began to fly, and what caused the dinosaurs to become extinct.

Pouch or No Pouch. Douglas S. Fox. *Discover*, v. 25 pp68–75 July 2004.

A tiny fossil jawbone found in Australia may upend a long-standing theory about where some of the earliest mammals originated and how they colonized the world, Fox writes. Until now, biologists have assumed that marsupial mammals prospered in Australia because they were isolated from competition with placental mammals. Now, however, Tom Rich of Monash University in Melbourne argues that a 115-million-year-old fossil jawbone, found at Flat Rocks in southeast Australia, shows that placental mammals were present in Australia eons earlier than previously thought and that they may even have competed with marsupials and lost. Rich and his colleagues hypothesize that placental mammals originated on the southern part of the ancient continent of Gondwanaland and moved north during the continent's breakup.

Useless Body Parts. Jocelyn Selim. *Discover*, v. 25 pp42–5 June 2004.

The body has a number of parts that are not needed, Selim explains. Some of these anatomical features are vanishing leftovers from man's prehominid ancestors, such as muscles useful for walking on all fours or hanging from trees that occur in various atrophied forms. Others are by-products of the natural redundancy of human sexual development—examples include nipples on men and the tiny vestigial sperm ducts behind the ovaries of women. Finally, there are others that, having outlived their usefulness, remain because there is no reason to leave, such as hair on the little toe.

Whose Life Would You Save? Carl Zimmer. *Discover*, v. 25 pp60–5 April 2004.

Morality may be hardwired into the human brain by evolution, reports Zimmer. Recent research suggests that, rather than using the power of reason alone, people pondering moral dilemmas are powerfully influenced by emotions that trigger instinctive responses that are the product of millions of years of evolution. Morality may have originated as a sense of fairness that would have helped early primates cooperate; as mankind's ancestors became more self-aware and acquired language, they transformed their feelings into moral codes that were passed on to their children. Studies indicate that personal moral decisions tend to stimulate certain parts of the brain more than impersonal moral decisions, with the latter triggering many of the same parts of the brain as nonmoral questions do. It may be that the brain regions stimulated by moral decision making are part of a neural network that produces the emotional instincts behind many of people's moral judgments.

What Do Females Want?: Impact of Feminism upon Darwinist Theory. Jessica Siegel. *Ms.*, v. 15 pp48–9 Spring 2005.

Darwinian feminists are offering evidence as to what women want, writes Siegel. For a good 100 years, evolutionary scientists overlooked the importance of female animals' behavior by treating it as a type of passive constant in a drama driven by aggressive males competing for sex. Now, scientists have painstakingly gathered evidence to prove that female animals play as active a part in evolution as do males. Today's studies, from apes in the wild to flies in the laboratory, reveal nature's remarkably complicated female politics, in which rank, sociability, mate choice, multiple-mating, competition, and infanticide all play a role in reproduction, child survival, and the way in which genes and behavior are passed to the next generation.

Was Darwin Wrong? David Quammen. *National Geographic*, v. 206 pp2–35 November 2004.

Evolution by natural selection, the central idea of the life's work of Charles Darwin, is a theory about the origin of adaptation, complexity, and diversity among the living creatures on Earth. According to Quammen, evolutionary theory is such a dangerously wonderful and wide-reaching perception of life that some find it unacceptable, despite the existence of a huge body of supporting evidence. According to a February 2001 Gallup poll, only 37 percent of the Americans polled were satisfied with the idea of a divine force behind the process of evolution, and only 12 percent believed that humans evolved from other forms of life without the involvement of a god. Evolution, however, is more crucial to human welfare, medical science, and the understanding of the world than ever, writes Quammen. Darwin's theories are detailed.

Evolution in Action. Jonathan Weiner. *Natural History*, v. 114 pp47–51 November 2005.

Evolution by natural selection can be observed in action throughout the natural world, Weiner says. Darwin thought of evolution as a process too slow to be observed. Biologists have since realized that evolution by natural selection can happen quickly enough to watch. Modern field studies are exploding, with more than 250 people around the world observing and documenting evolution in finches, guppies, aphids, flies, grayling, monkey flowers, salmon, and sticklebacks. Some workers are even documenting pairs of species that are coevolving. Others are studying evolution experimentally in the bacterium *Escherichia coli*.

The Illusion of Design. Richard Dawkins. *Natural History*, v. 114 pp35–7 November 2005.

Dawkins argues that evolution is a fact, not a theory. Charles Darwin discovered a means by which, without any external assistance, the laws of physics could, over geologically long periods of time, produce biological systems that appear to imitate intentional design. Natural selection insists that, rather than a specific form arising instantaneously, it came into being from a large number of small steps, each one of which is somewhat improbable but not ridiculously so, and, over countless generations, it takes this cumulative improbability to levels that exceed all sensible belief. This nonrandom cumulative ratcheting is not understood by many people, who believe that natural selection is a theory of chance. In their struggle to convince the public and their elected representatives that evolution is a fact, biologists must strive to explain the power of the cumulative ratcheting behind natural selection. Other barriers to accepting the fact of evolution, according to Dawkins, are people's reluctance to believe their relatedness to other animals and the mistaken association of evolution with social Darwinism.

The Origins of Form. Sean B. Carroll. *Natural History*, v. 114 pp58–63 November 2005.

Advances in the new science of evolutionary developmental biology, or evo-devo, have allowed biologists to explore the mechanisms that shape the diversity of organic forms, explains Carroll. After Darwin, research in all areas of biology led to the modern synthesis, which organized the fundamental principles that have guided evolutionary biology over the past 50 years. However, it has only been in the last 20 years that biologists have gained a revolutionary new understanding of how animal and plant forms and their complex structures arise and evolve. The key to this new understanding is development, which is intimately linked to evolution because all changes in form arise through changes in development. Carroll asserts that much of what has been learned in this new field of evo-devo has been so stunning and unexpected that it has dramatically expanded and re-formed the view of how evolution works. Simultaneously, evo-devo severely undermines the outmoded rhetoric of those who doubt that complex structures and organisms arise through natural selection.

Patterns. Niles Eldredge. *Natural History*, v. 114 p80 November 2005.

Eldredge explains that Darwin's theory of evolution arose from his observation of patterns in nature. During his famous voyage aboard the *Beagle*, Darwin noticed resemblances between fossil remains and modern species in South America, practically nonoverlapping distribution patterns of flightless birds on the same continent, and the existence of distinct forms of otherwise similar animals on the islands of the Galapagos archipelago. Returning to England a confirmed evolutionist, he looked for other patterns characteristic of evolution and found one in the Linnaean system for classifying plants and animals. Of the three patterns he observed on his voyage, Darwin reached a satisfactory explanation only for the different forms of animals on the Galapagos Islands, but the other patterns are now known also to comply with evolutionary theory.

Dinosaur Find Takes Scientists Beyond Bones. John Noble Wilford. *New York Times*, ppA1+ March 25, 2005.

Wilford notes that in Montana, scientists unearthed bones from a 70-million-year-old Tyrannosaurus Rex that showed traces of soft tissue and blood cells. Experts stated that the discovery may clarify the dinosaur's place in evolution, and its DNA could be extracted. Initial inspection of the tissue reveals that there is virtually no difference between the blood vessels of the dinosaur and those of the ostrich.

In Explaining Life's Complexity, Darwinists and Doubters Clash. Kenneth Chang. *New York Times*, ppA1+ August 22, 2005.

Proponents of intelligent design argue that it should be taught alongside evolution in the nation's schools as the complexity and diversity of life go beyond what evolution can explain, Chang writes. Mainstream scientists feel the claims of intelligent design run counter to a century of research supporting the explanatory and predictive power of Darwinian evolution. This article is part of the series A Debate over Darwin.

Less Jaw, Big Brain: Evolution Milestone Laid to Gene Flaw. John Noble Wilford. *New York Times* ppA1+ March 25, 2004.

Recent research has concluded that 2.4 million years ago a muscle gene underwent a disabling alteration that may have led to the enlarged brains of the lineage that evolved into modern humans, Wilford explains.

Scientists Speak Up on Mix of God and Science. Cornelia Dean. *New York Times*, ppA1+ August 23, 2005.

Scientists who embrace religion are beginning to speak out about their faith as religious groups challenge them in fields as various as evolution in the classroom, AIDS prevention, and stem cell research, Dean reports. Though they embrace religious faith, these scientists also embrace science, looking to the natural world for explanations of natural phenomena and recognizing that scientific ideas must often be overturned because of evidence from experimentation and observation. This belief in science separates them from those who endorse creationism or its doctrinal cousin, intelligent design, both of which depend on the existence of a supernatural force. Their belief in God challenges scientists who disdain religion and regard religious belief as little more than magical thinking. Their faith also challenges believers who stigmatize science as a godless enterprise and scientists as secular elitists.

When Cosmologies Collide. Judith Shulevitz. *The New York Times Book Review*, v. 111 pp10–11 January 22, 2006.

Shulevitz considers the possibility that something as trivial as scientists' lack of self-awareness may partly explain why, almost 150 years after Darwin, creationism in its different forms has become the most widespread critique of science. In this regard, it is worth considering how scientists usually react when evolution is attacked. Rather that attempting to view creationism as a culturally significant phenomenon, they tend to approach it as a set of ridiculous claims easily blown apart by science. This strategy is represented at its most effective and least controversial in Eugenie C. Scott's *Evolution Vs. Creationism*, which contains a straightforward history of the debate and essays written by partisans on both sides. To further understand why creationism is still thriving, one should refer to Michael Ruse's *The Evolution-Creation Struggle*.

80 Years of Watching the Evolutionary Scenery. Ernst Mayr, *Science*, v. 305 pp46–7 July 2, 2004.

On his 100th birthday, Mayr recounts his experiences from the 1920s to the 1950s, crucial years in the history of evolutionary biology.

Changes in the Air. Sid Perkins. *Science News*, v. 168 pp395–6 December 17, 2005.

Evidence suggests that changes in atmospheric oxygen levels have a great impact on the evolution of animals, writes Perkins. Geologic periods defined by high atmospheric oxygen concentrations had high levels of biological innovation, but biodiversity waned whenever oxygen concentrations fell precipitously. Recent laboratory experiments have shown that insects raised in oxygen-rich environments can attain larger proportions in just a few generations and that variations in oxygen abundance can affect the development of reptiles. Such experiments suggest that a precipitous drop in atmospheric oxygen could severely test animals that need high concentrations of oxygen to fuel an active lifestyle. This theory is bolstered by evidence from the fossil record, with some of Earth's mass extinctions occurring during or after geologically sudden drops in atmospheric oxygen. Oxygen concentrations and flora and fauna at various points in geological time are described.

The Fossil Fallacy. Michael Shermer. *Scientific American*, v. 292 p32 March 2005.

Shermer asserts that creationists' demand for fossils that represent so-called missing links demonstrates a deep misunderstanding of science. In debates over the theory of evolution, creationists often request evidence of a single fossil that constitutes proof of a multifarious process or historical sequence. Proof of evolution, however, comes from such diverse fields as geology, paleontology, biogeography, comparative anatomy and physiology, molecular biology, and genetics. Together, these fields reveal that life evolved in a certain sequence by a particular process.

It's Dogged as Does It: Darwin and His Discoveries on Galapagos. Michael Shermer. *Scientific American*, v. 294 pp34–5 February 2006.

Retracing Charles Darwin's footsteps in the Galapagos reveals how revolutions in science actually evolve, Shermer suggests. The iconic myth is that Darwin left the Galapagos as an evolutionist, having discovered natural selection operating on finch beaks and tortoise shells. Frank J. Sulloway, a historian of science at the University of California, Berkeley, and the writer retraced Darwin's footsteps in an attempt to determine how he really established the theory of evolution. Based on studies of Darwin's notes and journals, Sulloway maintains that Darwin returned from his trip as a creationist and dates Darwin's acceptance of evolution to the second week of March 1837, following a meeting with the eminent ornithologist John Gould, who had been studying his Galapagos bird specimens. This is quite different from the myth that science proceeds by select so-called eureka discoveries followed by sudden revolutionary revelations.

Evolution and the ID Wars. *Skeptical Inquirer*, v. 29 pp32–60 November/ December 2005.

Among the topics discussed in this article are the lack of a logical foundation for Professor Michael Behe's concept of irreducible complexity and the way opponents of evolution are framing the issues of the debate to their own advantage. The article also looks at the deliberate misquoting by ID proponents of scientists to make it wrongly appear as though they have serious reservations about evolution. Finally, it covers how advances in embryology and evolutionary development biology have profoundly reshaped scientists' picture of how evolution works.

Why Scientists Get So Angry When Dealing with ID Proponents. Jason Rosenhouse. *Skeptical Inquirer*, v. 29 pp42–5 November/December 2005.

Rosenhouse argues that ID advocates are constantly quoting scientists out of context to make it wrongly look as though they have serious reservations about evolution. In dozens of cases examined, the quotations were massively out of context. Sometimes what was presented as a small revision of an arcane part of evolutionary theory was exaggerated into a criticism of the theory in its entirety. On other occasions, the meaning of a statement was so twisted that it was made to appear to be saying the precise opposite of the author's clearly stated intention. In every case, the quotation was made to appear to mean something different from the writer's actual opinion. The writer examines a particular example in which the words of paleontologist Peter Ward are taken out of context by ID proponent William Dembski.

New Human Species Found in Indonesia. *Society*, v. 42 pp5–6 January/February 2005.

Archaeologists have discovered a lost world of small archaic humans in Indonesia, the magazine reports. In the latest edition of *Nature*, paleoanthropologist Peter Brown and archaeologist Michael Morwood of the University of New England in Armidale, Australia, and their colleagues at the Indonesian Centre for Archaeology in Jakarta, Indonesia, describe the remains of an adult skull and partial skeleton that were discovered in 2004 in the Liang Bua Cave on the tropical island of Flores. This cave woman and the isolated bones of a number of other individuals are so unlike modern humans—the partial skeleton was just one meter in height—that the researchers christened them as a new species, *Homo floresiensis*. These small humans hunted dwarf elephants and Komodo dragons on Flores at the same time that modern humans lived on nearby islands and were circumnavigating the globe.

Darwin Would Have Loved It: How Tiktaalik Rosae Fits Within Framework of Evolutionary Theory. Michael J. Novacek. *Time*, v. 167 p60 April 17, 2006.

Fossils are the only direct evidence of how life has developed since the first rudimentary cells emerged on Earth some 3.6 billion years ago, explains Novacek. Unfortunately, the fossil record is not complete, a reality that Charles Darwin would have recognized, but he would have been very pleased to see the fascinating discoveries made by paleontologists in the 150 years since then. Many people who reject evolution in favor of divine creation insist that the fossil record does not contain the so-called transitional species anticipated by Darwin's theory, but the walking fish Tiktaalik is further proof that such an argument is utterly incorrect: All kinds of missing links preserved in minute detail have been and will be discovered. The writer discusses the continued importance of Darwin's evolutionary theory.

Forbidden Fruit. Peter Gilmour. *U.S. Catholic*, v. 70 p6 April 2005.

Pierre Teilhard de Chardin, a Jesuit priest from France who died 50 years ago on April 10, not only believed in biological evolution, but also believed that it was a crucial and central dynamic of divine activity, says Gilmour. His life in exile demanded by church authorities gave him the opportunity to further develop and advance his evolutionary theory and theology. He penned a number of theologically oriented texts, but church authorities prohibited any of them from being published. He handed his theological manuscripts to his secretary and friend, Rhoda de Terra, assuring their eventual publication after his demise. Subsequently, his books became famous, and on the 50th anniversary of his death, many celebrations are planned to mark his life.

Darwin's Worms. Amy Stewart. *The Wilson Quarterly*, v. 28 pp48–58 Winter 2004.

With his book *The Formation of Vegetable Mould, through the Action of Worms, with Observations on Their Habits* (1881), Charles Darwin came to the realization, unprecedented among scientists, that earthworms could bring about gradual geological changes over long periods of time. At the time, writes Stewart, many people still believed that earthworms were a garden pest that harmed plant roots and ruined clean green lawns with their castings. After a visit to the home of his uncle, Darwin realized that earthworms were responsible for the rich uppermost layer of soil, then known as "vegetable mould." This idea that the smallest changes could lead to huge outcomes fits perfectly with Darwin's work on evolution and the origin of species.

Index

Acanthostega, 103
ACLU (American Civil Liberties Union),
    45, 51
Adler, Jerry, 9–14
Ahlberg, Erik, 106
Alberts, Bruce, 41
Altevogt, John, 52–54
Ambrose, Stanley, 134
Ambulocetus, 108–109
American Museum of Natural History,
    77–78, 79
amphibians, 102
Apesteguia, Sebastian, 115
aquatic animals, 100–103
archaean genealogy, 78, 82–83
Archaeopteryx, 99, 102, 106

bacterial flagella, 56–59
bacterial genealogy, 78, 82–83
Bajpai, Sunil, 108–109
Balanced Treatment for Creation-Sci-
    ence and Evolution-Science Act, 15,
    162, 164
Baldauf, Sandra, 78
Barnes, Lawrence, 111, 113
Begley, Sharon, 145–147
Behe, Michael, 36–37, 56–59, 66
birds, 102, 128
blogs, 49
Blombos Cave, 137–139, 141–142
blood clotting, 57–58
Bonsell, Alan, 38
Boudreaux, Edward, 161
Boyd, Robert, 127
Boyles, Denis, 51–54
brain size, 89, 126–128, 143
    See also cognitive capacity
Branch, Glenn, 39–50
Brennan, William J., Jr., 158–162
Broad Institute, 91
Brochier, Celine, 84
Brooks, Alison, 135
Brownlee, Karin, 54
Buchanan, Pat, 46–47

Buckingham, William, 38
Buitreraptor, 114–116
Bunn, Henry, 144
Bush, George W., 40, 42

Carroll, Robert, 106
Carroll, Sean, 88
Chadwick, Douglas, 107–113
chimpanzees, 89, 91–93
Circe network, 77–79
Clack, Jennifer, 106
cognitive capacity, 125–130, 133–142
Collins, Francis, 13–14
computer analyses, 73, 77–79
Conklin-Brittain, NancyLou, 143
Contact, 59–61
Cook, Gareth, 87–93
Cook, Jill, 141
cooking, 143–144
Correns, Carl, 18
court rulings, 15, 155–157, 158–165
creationism
    court rulings, 15, 38
    intelligent design (ID) as a form of,
        27–28, 39–41, 156
Creationism Act, 158–164
creative intelligence, 134–135
Crick, Francis, 19–21
CRSC (Center for the Renewal of Science
    and Culture), 65
cultural modernity, 133–142, 143–144,
    145–147
cultural transmission, 128

d'Errico, Francesco, 138
Daeschler, Edward, 105
Darwin, Charles, 9–14, 15, 62–65
Darwin, Erasmus, 5–8, 11
Darwin's finches, 62–65, 88–89
Darwinian threshold, 86
Darwinism, 10, 41, 43, 47
    See also natural selection, theory of
Dawkins, Richard, 13
de Vries, Hugo, 18
de Waal, Frans, 131–132

Deacon, Hilary, 136
Dembski, William, 37, 59–62, 65–66
Descent of Man, The (Darwin), 12
Di Giulio, Massimo, 84–85
Diamond, Jared, 117–120
diet, 143–144
dinosaurs, 102, 114–116
Discovery Institute, 41
divergence times, 93
DNA (deoxyribose nucleic acid), 81–86
 discovery of structure, 19–21
 evolution, 84–85
Doebley, John, 89
Domning, Daryl, 101
Doolittle, Russell, 58
dromaeosaurs, 114–116

education
 as political/religious debate, 65–66
 controversies, 51–54
 court rulings, 15, 155–157, 158–165
 media coverage, 39–49
Edwards v. Aguillard, 158–165
Eldredge, Niles, 10
Epperson v. Arkansas, 160–161
eukaryote genealogy, 78, 82–83
evolutionary developmental biology, 88–90
evolutionary synthesis, 71–72
evolutionary theories
 evolutionary developmental biology, 88–90
 evolutionary synthesis, 71–72
 Harris Poll, 27–34
 neutral theory of molecular evolution, 73–74
 See also intelligent design (ID); natural selection, theory of

family trees, 73, 77–80
finches, 62–65, 88–89
fish, 102
flagella, bacterial, 56–59
Flores Island, 117–120
Forrest, Barbara, 65–66
Forterre, Patrick, 83
fossil records
 dinosaurs, 114–116
 micropygmies, 117–120
 transitional forms, 99–104, 105–106

whales, 107–113
Fox, Terry, 44–45
Franklin, Rosalind, 19–21
fruit flies, 62–65, 126
Funk, Daniel, 75
Futuyma, Douglas J., 71–76

Galapagos Islands, 11, 62
gene expression, 87–88
 See also evolutionary developmental biology
gene mutations, 71–75, 88–89
gene transfer, 84
genealogy
 chimpanzee research, 91–93
 family trees, 73, 77–80
 LUCA, 81–86
genetic drift, 73
genome-sequencing projects, 83–84
Gerald Parshall, 19–22
Goedert, James, 110–111
Goodstein, Laurie, 35–38
Gould, Stephen Jay, 13
Grant, Michael, 45–46
Grant, Peter and Rosemary, 62–64
Green, Harry, 79

Hamilton, Garry, 81–86
Hardball episode, 44–45
Harris Poll, 27–34
Hayden, Thomas, 77–80
Hemenway, Bob, 52–54
Henshilwood, Christopher, 133, 137–142
heredity, 16–18, 71–72
hippopotami, 113
Homo erectus, 143–144
Hooker, Joseph, 15
horizontal gene transfer, 84
horses, 100
Hovers, Erelia, 141
Howarth, William, 13
HOX genes, 64–65
Hubby, John, 73
Huxley, Thomas, 12, 15
hybridization, 92–93
hyperthermophiles, 84

Ichthyostega, 102
innovation, 128–130, 134–135
intelligence. *See* cognitive capacity
intelligent design (ID), 27–28
 about, 14, 15, 55

as form of creationism, 39–41, 156
as political/religious debate, 65–66
characteristic signature of, 59–62
irreducible complexity and, 56–59
media coverage, 39–49
natural causation in, 62–65

Janies, Dan, 78
Jenkins, Farish, 105
John Paul II, 15
Johnson, Phillip, 65
Jones, John E., 35–38
journalism. *See* media coverage

Kansas, 27, 38, 51, 65
Kawecki, Tadeusz, 126
Keith, Bill, 160, 161, 164–165
Kimura, Motoo, 73–74
King-Hele, Desmond, 5–8
Kirschner, Marc, 88
Kitzmiller v. Dover Area School District,
    35–38, 155–157
Kitzmiller, Tammy, 37
Klein, Richard, 134
Koonin, Eugene, 86
Krische, Vince, 53

Laden, Greg, 143–144
Laland, Kevin, 128
language, 134, 140–142, 145–147
Lefebvre, Louis, 128–129
Lemon v. Kurtzman, 159, 163
Lewis, Edward, 64
Lewontin, Richard, 73
LUCA (last universal common ancestor),
    81–86

Maestro, Vittorio, 55–66
Makovicky, Peter, 114–116
Malthus, Thomas, 12
mammals, 101–102
Matthews, Chris, 44–45
McBrearty, Sally, 135–136, 138–139
media coverage, 39–49
Mendel, Gregor Johann, 16–18, 71
Mery, Frederic, 126
Meyer, Stephen, 41–42
microcephaly, 90
micropygmies, 117–120
Miller, Geoffrey, 128, 145
Miller, Kenneth, 37, 57–59
Milner, Richard, 55–66

Mirecki, Paul, 52–54
mirror self-recognition, 131–132
Mithen, Steven, 145–146
modern synthesis theory. *See* evolution-
    ary synthesis
Mohler Al, 46–47
Monastersky, Richard, 105–106
"Monkey Trial", 15, 51
monkeys, 131–132
Mooney, Chris, 40
mouse traps, 56–59
Mullen, William, 114–116
music, 145–147

natural selection, theory of
    about, 12
    irreducible complexity and, 56–59
    natural causation in, 62–65
    significance in evolutionary biology,
        71–72
    See also Darwinism
Neanderthals, 135, 138, 141, 145–147
neutral theory of molecular evolution, 73–
    74
newsmagazine coverage, 42–44, 47
newspaper coverage, 41–42, 47
Newsweek, 43
Newton, Isaac, 61–62
Nisbet, Matthew, 40
No Child Left Behind Act, 66
Norell, Mark, 114
Nosil, Patrick, 75
Novacek, Michael, 79

O'Leary, Maureen, 79
O'Reilly Factor, The, 45–46
ochre processing, 136–137, 141
Of Pandas and People, 38, 155
Okada, Norihiro, 113
Origin of Species, The (Darwin), 9–10

Pakicetus, 108
paleontology. *See* fossil records
Paley, William, 55
Palmer, Jeffrey, 42
Parshall, Gerald, 19–21
Pauling, Linus, 20
Pennock, Robert, 60–62
Philippe, Herve, 84
phylogeny, 77–78
Pilbeam, David, 91–92
Poole, Anthony, 81, 85

population growth, 139–140
prokaryote genealogy, 82–83
Prothero, Donald, 99–104

Randerson, James, 143–144
Reader, Simon, 125–130
Rehm, Christy, 37
Reich, David, 91–92
religion
    evolution stance, 11, 12–13, 48, 156
    fundamentalism and evolution, 42
    instruction in public schools, 15
    John Paul II on evolution, 15
reptiles, 101–102
Reville, William, 16–18
Richerson, Peter, 127
RNA (ribonucleic acid), 82, 84–85
Rolston, Holmes, III, 13–14
Rood, Michael, 146
Rosenhouse, Jason, 39–50

Scalia, Antonin, 162–165
Scarborough Country, 46–47
schools. *See* education
science education
    as political/religious debate, 65–66
    controversies, 51–54
    court rulings, 155–157, 158–165
    media coverage, 39–49
Scopes, John, 15, 51
Scott, Eugenie, 38, 44–45, 63–65
SETI (Search for Extraterrestrial Intelligence), 59–61
sexual selection, 75–76, 127–128
Sharktooth Hill, 111–112
Shubin, Neil, 105–106
Sol, Daniel, 129
SOMA (Society of Open-minded Atheists and Agnostics), 52–54
speciation, 72, 74–76, 92–93
Supreme Court, U.S., 15, 158–165
symbolism, 134, 137–138, 140–142, 145–147
synthetic theory of evolution. *See* evolutionary synthesis

Tabin, Cliff, 89
Tasmania, 118, 140
television coverage, 44–47
Temple of Nature, The (Darwin), 7–8
Thewissen, Hans, 108–109
Tiktaalik, 105–106
Time magazine article, 43–44
Toumai, 92
Trehub, Sandra, 146
Tschermak-Seysenegg, Erich von, 18
Twain, Mark, 151–154

universal tree of life, 77–80
    See also family tree
University of Kansas, 51–54
USA Today article, 41–42

vertebrates, 103–104

Wade, Nicholas, 131–132
Walczak, Witold, 37
Wallace v. Jaffree, 160
Wallace, Alfred Russell, 71
Walsh, Christopher, 89–90
Warren, Earl, 15
Washington Post article, 42
Watson, James, 19–21
Weblogs, 49
Wells, Jonathan, 62–65, 66
whales, 100–101, 107–113
Wheeler, Ward, 78–79
White, Randall, 138, 140–141
Wilberforce, Samuel, 12, 15
Wilkins, Maurice, 20–21
Wilson, Edward, 10, 79–80
Woese, Carl, 78, 82, 85–86
Wong, Kate, 133–142
Wrangham, Richard, 143–144
Wray, Gregory, 87

Yellen, John, 136

Zoonomia, 6–7